The
ESSENTIAL GUIDE TO
BIBLE
PROPHECY

TIM LaHAYE
ED HINDSON

HARVEST HOUSE PUBLISHERS
EUGENE, OREGON

Cover by Dugan Design Group, Bloomington, Minnesota

Cover photo © Songquan Deng / Shutterstock

TIM LAHAYE PROPHECY LIBRARY is a series trademark of Tim F. LaHaye and Beverly J. LaHaye. Harvest House Publishers, Inc., is the exclusive licensee of the trademark TIM LAHAYE PROPHECY LIBRARY.

Some material has been adapted from *The Popular Bible Prophecy Workbook*.

THE ESSENTIAL GUIDE TO BIBLE PROPHECY
Copyright © 2006/2012 by Pre-Trib Research Center, Tim LaHaye, and Ed Hindson
Published by Harvest House Publishers
Eugene, Oregon 97402
www.harvesthousepublishers.com

Library of Congress Cataloging-in-Publication Data

LaHaye, Tim F.
The essential guide to Bible prophecy / Tim LaHaye and Ed Hindson.
    p. cm.
Includes bibliographical references.
ISBN 978-0-7369-3784-9 (pbk.)
ISBN 978-0-7369-4262-1 (eBook)
1. Bible—Prophecies. I. Hindson, Edward E. II. Title.
BS647.3.L33 2012
220.1'5—dc23
                                2012019549

Printed in the United States of America

12 13 14 15 16 17 18 19 20 / VP-NI / 10 9 8 7 6 5 4 3 2 1

CONTENTS

WHAT DOES THE FUTURE HOLD?

Everyone is curious about the future. We all want to know what is going to happen next, but only God has the ability to see what is to come. Therefore, we must rely on His Word as our guide to understanding what lies ahead.

We are living in incredible times. Things are changing so fast we can hardly keep up with them. Before we can catch our breath, we are hurried on to the next significant event on the horizon. Tensions in the Middle East, the development of weapons of mass destruction, and threats to global peace fill the newspaper headlines. We all sense that the world is moving toward some great climax.

People today are asking, where are we headed? What will happen next? And how can we be prepared? These are the very questions Bible prophecy answers for us. Prophecy helps us to see into the future with clarity and confidence.

The purpose of Bible prophecy is not to frighten us, but to assure us that God is in control. In times of human uncertainty, we can rest assured that we have a "sure word of prophecy" (2 Peter 1:19 KJV) that shines like a beacon of light into the darkness of our times. Therefore, we can lift our heads and know that our redemption is drawing near (Luke 21:28).

The purpose of this study is to help us examine what the Bible says about the future. We will look at key Bible prophecies about such matters as the rapture of the church and the rise of the Antichrist. We will explore major prophetic passages that describe the Tribulation, Christ's glorious appearing, the millennial kingdom, and heaven.

The hope of the second coming of Christ is a strong encouragement for us to live right. The Bible reminds us, "Abide in Him, that when He appears, we may have confidence and not be ashamed before Him at His coming...We know that when He is revealed, we shall be like Him, for we shall see Him as He is. And everyone who has this hope in Him purifies himself, just as He is pure" (1 John 2:28; 3:2-3).

God bless you as you study these great prophetic truths. May they challenge your mind, move your heart, and lift your soul with great anticipation for the Savior's return.

Tim LaHaye
Ed Hindson

1

Only God Can Prophesy

The uniqueness of God is expressed in the predictive nature of Bible prophecy. There is nothing like this in any other religion. Only the God of the Bible can predict the future with perfect accuracy. "For I am God, and there is no other...declaring the end from the beginning, and from ancient times things that are not yet done...Indeed I have spoken it; I will also bring it to pass" (Isaiah 46:9-11).

Jesus Christ also claimed divine authority for the prophetic Scriptures. The most dramatic prophecies in all the Bible point to the coming Messiah-Savior, who would both suffer and reign. These ancient prophecies were so precisely fulfilled that there can be no serious doubt that they point to only one person who has ever lived—Jesus of Nazareth.

After His resurrection, Jesus told His disciples, "All things must be fulfilled which were written in the Law of Moses and the Prophets and the Psalms concerning Me" (Luke 24:44). Christ Himself then taught the disciples which Old Testament scriptures predicted

His life and ministry. "He opened their understanding that they might comprehend the Scriptures" (verse 45).

The New Testament writers were instructed by the Lord Himself regarding biblical prophecies and their fulfillment. The threefold designation—Law, Prophets, and Psalms—refers to the three major divisions of the Hebrew Bible. Jesus was specifically stating that the entire Old Testament predicted the details of His life, ministry, death, and resurrection. Therefore, the preaching of the early Christian disciples was filled with references to Old Testament prophecies and their fulfillment in the person of Jesus Christ (see Acts 2:25-36; 3:22-23; 4:25-26; 13:46-49).

During His earthly ministry, Jesus was recognized as a prophet of God (Matthew 21:11; Luke 7:16) and a teacher from God (John 3:2). Jesus even referred to Himself as a prophet (Matthew 13:57; Luke 13:33). The early preaching of the apostles also emphasized the prophetic nature of Christ's ministry (Acts 3:24-26; 7:37). Matthew's Gospel alone makes 65 references to Old Testament scriptures, emphasizing their fulfillment in Christ.

The Prophet and the Prophetic Ministry

The prophetic histories are followed in the Hebrew canon by the prophetic books of prediction. The two form a unit in the middle portion of the threefold canon, under the common term Prophets. Jewish readers distinguish them as the "former prophets" and "latter prophets." The manner of speaking by the prophets may be best characterized as preaching. Their messages also included symbolic actions (2 Kings 13:17-19), object lessons (Jeremiah 1:11-14), and written sermons (Jeremiah 36:4).

The Hebrew prophets were men of God who preached God's Word and also predicted the future. Their messages revealed events that were yet to come. In this regard, their messages were supernatural, not natural. They were derived neither from observation nor

8

intellectual thought, but from knowing God and speaking with Him.

What is a prophet? The first person in the Bible to be called a prophet was Abraham. This was a title given to him by God (Genesis 20:6-7). There were likely prophets who served before Abraham, such as Enoch (compare Genesis 5:24 with Jude 14), but it is significant that Abraham is the first prophet explicitly mentioned in Scripture. From his life, we can observe two key traits of the biblical prophets.

First, God chooses a prophet. Abraham's call makes this clear:

> The LORD had said to Abram, "Go from your country, your people and your father's household to the land I will show you.
> "I will make you into a great nation,
>   and I will bless you;
> I will make your name great,
>   and you will be a blessing.
> I will bless those who bless you,
>   and whoever curses you I will curse;
> and all peoples on earth
>   will be blessed through you" (Genesis 12:1-3 NIV).

Abraham's role as a prophet was not a vocation he sought. Rather, it was a result of God's unique, sovereign calling upon his life.

Second, a prophet is a person with God's message. God called Abraham to serve Him by revealing God's message to others. Moses, who would also later serve as a prophet, likewise revealed God's message by receiving the law of the Lord for the people of Israel. Other Old Testament prophets would look to both Abraham and Moses as examples of their role as people called by God to communicate the message of the Lord to those who needed it.

The revelation of God to the prophet is a process by which God reveals His secrets to the prophet (Amos 3:7). The term "reveal" (Hebrew, *galah*) means to "uncover," as in "uncovering the ear" (1 Samuel 9:15). Thus, when God "uncovers" the prophet's ear, He reveals what has been previously hidden (as in 2 Samuel 7:27) so that the prophet perceives what the Lord has said (Jeremiah 23:18).

A prophet's message is not the product of human effort. Rather, biblical prophecy finds its origin in the Spirit of God. "Above all, you must understand that no prophecy of Scripture came about by the prophet's own interpretation of things. For prophecy never had its origin in the human will, but prophets, though human, spoke from God as they were carried along by the Holy Spirit" (2 Peter 1:20-21 NIV).

These verses indicate several specific details related to the revelation of God. First, prophecy is completely *from* God: "No prophecy of Scripture came about by the prophet's own interpretation of things." Second, prophecy is completely *of* God: "Prophecy never had its origin in the human will." Third, prophecy is communicated *through God's prophets*: "Prophets, though human, spoke from God." Fourth, prophets were *guided by God's Spirit*: "Prophets, though human, spoke from God as they were carried along by the Holy Spirit." In every way, Scripture makes clear that biblical prophecy is a work of God through prophets of God to communicate God's message.

Another consideration is the relationship of prophecy to the Bible as a whole. It has been estimated that 27 percent of the Bible includes prophecy. In other words, approximately one-fourth of the Bible is prophetic. If the Bible is considered authoritative and perfect, then the prophecies of the Bible encompass a large portion of God's perfectly revealed Scripture.

What does the Bible teach regarding the nature of the Scriptures? A brief look expresses a clear view that the words of the Bible are indeed perfect. For example, consider Psalm 19:7-11 (NIV):

> The law of the LORD is perfect,
>> refreshing the soul.
> The statutes of the LORD are trustworthy,
>> making wise the simple.
> The precepts of the LORD are right,
>> giving joy to the heart.
> The commands of the LORD are radiant,
>> giving light to the eyes.
> The fear of the LORD is pure,
>> enduring forever.
> The decrees of the LORD are firm,
>> and all of them are righteous.
>
> They are more precious than gold,
>> than much pure gold;
> they are sweeter than honey,
>> than honey from the honeycomb.
> By them your servant is warned;
>> in keeping them there is great reward.

In 2 Timothy 3:16-17 (NIV), Paul called Scripture "God-breathed." We have seen that Peter taught that prophets were controlled by God's Spirit. Jesus Himself agreed with this high view of Scripture:

> Do not think that I have come to abolish the Law or the Prophets; I have not come to abolish them but to fulfill them. For truly I tell you, until heaven and earth disappear, not the smallest letter, not the least stroke of a pen, will by any means disappear from the Law until everything is accomplished (Matthew 5:17-18 NIV).

Here, Jesus made clear that His incarnation and ministry were fulfillments of Old Testament writings. In making this statement, He indicated that the Old Testament authors were inspired by God and accurately spoke of His coming.

It is obvious, therefore, that the Spirit of God is necessary for prophetic inspiration. Thus, it was by the Spirit that the Word of the Lord was communicated to the prophet and by the Spirit that the Word was mediated to the people.

Messianic Prophecy

The high aspirations of the Old Testament writers and their application of God-like characteristics to a coming prince, the Messiah, the son of David, compel us to see one who is more than a mere man. He was called both the son of David and the Son of God.

The New Testament based its entire apologetic on the facts that Jesus was the Messiah predicted in the Old Testament and that these predictions were conclusively fulfilled in Jesus' life. The New Testament recognizes the value of using predictive prophecy and its fulfillment as apologetic evidence to prove that Christianity is supernatural and credible.

Jesus Himself repeatedly taught that these prophecies "must be fulfilled." Under God's direction, He subjected Himself completely to the course they charted, and He considered the details of His life and death as events that must take place because they were written in the Word of God. The purpose of messianic prophecy was to make the Messiah known after He had fulfilled the events foretold. These prophecies served as preparatory devices that signaled His arrival.

The New Testament writers insisted that Jesus was the Christ on the basis of three essential arguments:

1. Jesus' resurrection
2. eyewitness accounts of what happened
3. fulfillment of Old Testament prophecies

Within weeks of the resurrection, the early Christians were proclaiming the events in Jesus' life as fulfillments of specific prophecies.

In the first Christian sermon, Peter announced, "This is what was spoken by the prophet Joel...David says concerning Him...[God] would raise up the Christ to sit on [David's] throne, he, foreseeing this, spoke concerning the resurrection of the Christ" (Acts 2:16, 25,30-31).

In following this line of proof, the apostles did what God's prophets had done for centuries. They pointed to the fulfillment of prophecy as the ultimate proof of the truthfulness of God's Word. In so doing, they urged their listeners to believe the whole message of the gospel of Jesus Christ.

Prophecies Fulfilled in the Life of Christ

The Old Testament is filled with prophecies about the human race, the nation of Israel, and future events in general. And the most important prophecies are those that point to the coming of Christ. These are not merely isolated "proof texts"; the whole of the Old Testament points the way to a coming future Messiah.

Even before the time of Jesus, the Jews recognized that many of these predictions were messianic. Here are ten examples:

Prophecy	Subject	Fulfillment
Genesis 3:15 "her Seed"	**seed of a woman**	**Galatians 4:4** "born of a woman"
Genesis 12:3 "All the families of the earth shall be blessed."	**descendant of Abraham**	**Matthew 1:1** "the Son of Abraham"
Genesis 49:10 "The scepter shall not depart from Judah."	**tribe of Judah**	**Luke 3:33** "the son of Judah"
Isaiah 9:7 "upon the throne of David"	**heir of David**	**Luke 1:32** "the throne of His father David"

Prophecy	Subject	Fulfillment
Micah 5:2 "Bethlehem…out of you shall come…the One to be Ruler in Israel."	**born in Bethlehem**	**Luke 2:4-7** "the city of David, which is called Bethlehem… she brought forth her firstborn Son"
Isaiah 7:14 "The virgin shall conceive."	**born of a virgin**	**Matthew 1:23** "The virgin shall be with child."
Psalm 2:7 "You are My Son."	**declared the Son of God**	**Matthew 3:17** "This is My beloved Son."
Isaiah 53:3 "He is despised and rejected."	**rejected by his own**	**John 1:11** "His own did not receive Him."
Psalm 41:9 "my own familiar friend…against me"	**betrayed by a friend**	**Matthew 26:50** "Friend, why have you come?"
Zechariah 12:10 "on Me whom they pierced"	**death by crucifixion**	**Matthew 27:23** "Let Him be crucified!"

Another clear example is found in Matthew's account of the wise men.

"Where is the one who has been born king of the Jews? We saw his star when it rose and have come to worship him."

When King Herod heard this he was disturbed, and all Jerusalem with him. When he had called together all the people's chief priests and teachers of the law, he asked them where the Messiah was to be born.

"In Bethlehem in Judea," they replied, "for this is what the prophet has written:

"'But you, Bethlehem, in the land of Judah,
   are by no means least among the rulers of Judah;

> for out of you will come a ruler
> who will shepherd my people Israel'"
> (Matthew 2:5-6 NIV, quoting Micah 5:2-4).

These Jewish scholars were well aware of Micah's prophecy long before Jesus was revealed. Yet Micah had spoken these words 700 years earlier with explicit precision regarding the exact location of the Messiah's birth.

Luke's Gospel recalls a fulfilled Old Testament prophecy related to Christ's entry into Jerusalem on the day we call Palm Sunday.

> Those who were sent ahead went and found it just as he had told them. As they were untying the colt, its owners asked them, "Why are you untying the colt?"
> They replied, "The Lord needs it."
> They brought it to Jesus, threw their cloaks on the colt and put Jesus on it. As he went along, people spread their cloaks on the road (Luke 19:32-36 NIV).

What is the significance of Jesus entering the city on a young donkey? The Jewish prophet Zechariah wrote,

> Rejoice greatly, O Daughter of Zion!
> Shout, O Daughter of Jerusalem!
> Behold, your King is coming to you;
> He is just and having salvation,
> Lowly and riding on a donkey,
> A colt, the foal of a donkey (Zechariah 9:9).

Utilizing donkeys for travel was common during this time, but specifically referring to "a colt, the foal of a donkey" demonstrates a level of accuracy that appears to have no other explanation than predictive prophecy. Amazingly, Zechariah penned these words around 550 years before the event!

In yet another prophecy, Matthew shared the financial motivation behind Judas Iscariot's betrayal of Jesus: "Then one of the Twelve—the one called Judas Iscariot—went to the chief priests and asked, 'What are you willing to give me if I deliver him over to you?' So they counted out for him thirty pieces of silver" (Matthew 26:14-15 NIV).

Interestingly, Matthew, the former tax collector, noted that an Old Testament prophet had previously predicted this specific amount of money. God commanded Zechariah to "shepherd the flock marked for slaughter" (Zechariah 11:4). After a dispute about his work, he ended his shepherding (verses 8-9). In his exit interview with his employer, he remarked, "'If you think it best, give me my pay; but if not, keep it.' So they paid me thirty pieces of silver" (verse 12). This visual form of teaching served as a specific prophecy regarding the exact price the chief priests paid Judas Iscariot to betray Jesus.

These are just three of the approximately 120 distinct Old Testament prophecies of the first coming of Christ. They are like pieces of a puzzle. Each presents a distinct element of the Savior's life and ministry, but the whole picture portrayed by these pieces can be seen only after their fulfillment. Not until Jesus came did these prophecies come into clear relation with one another. The chances of all these prophecies being fulfilled in the life of one man is one chance in 84 followed by 131 zeroes.

These 120 prophecies of Christ's first coming are overwhelming evidence of the divine origin of Scripture, the messiahship of Jesus, and the truth of Christianity. When viewed as a whole, the collective impact of these prophecies and their fulfillment in the Gospels cannot be easily dismissed by unbelievers. Again, the mathematical possibility of all these predictions being fulfilled in one person is absolutely astounding.

Louis Lapides grew up in a Jewish family in New Jersey. During a time of reflection on his own spiritual journey, he realized that the description of the Messiah in Isaiah 53 perfectly fit the portrait of Jesus of Nazareth. Now a pastor, his studies and life experiences have led him from skepticism regarding messianic prophecies concerning Jesus to personally embracing Him as Messiah in his own life.

In an interview, Lapides was asked, "If the prophecies were so obvious to you and pointed so unquestionably toward Jesus, why don't more Jews accept Him as their Messiah?"

He answered, "In my case, I took the time to read them." In many cases, we undervalue the impact of the fulfilled prophecies regarding Jesus Christ because of our lack of study regarding how specifically the Bible has spoken. In our study together, we'll discover that Scripture has frequently spoken very specifically regarding many events, both those fulfilled in the past as well as those that are yet to be fulfilled.

What About Future Prophecies?

The accurate fulfillment of the prophecies of Christ's first coming point us to the certainty that the 300 prophecies of His second coming will also be fulfilled. Because the prophecies relating to Christ's first coming have been fulfilled literally, we can confidently expect that the prophecies relating to His second coming will be fulfilled equally as literally.

We have every reason to believe in the trustworthiness of the Bible's prophecies about the future, but we can accept them only by faith until the time of their fulfillment. And our faith in these prophecies is not based on a misplaced pious hope. Rather, it is based on the literal fulfillment of prophecies from the past. This alone gives us great confidence that the prophecies not yet fulfilled will indeed come to pass.

The fact that Bible prophecies have always been fulfilled in an exact and detailed manner assures us that, in regard to prophecies not yet fulfilled, Christ will come again just as He said (John 14:1-3).

We can look forward to the unfolding of the future because we know it is under God's sovereign control.

John's Gospel ends by reminding us that the "world itself could not contain" the books that could be written about Jesus Christ (John 21:25). But John himself, Jesus' personal disciple, states, "These are written that you may believe that Jesus is the Christ, the Son of God, and that believing you may have life in His name" (John 20:31).

Why Does Bible Prophecy Matter?

All prophecy is important today for several reasons. This is the clear teaching of the New Testament.

Studying unfulfilled prophecy is useful. Paul wrote in 2 Timothy 3:16-17 (NIV), "All Scripture is God-breathed and is useful for teaching, rebuking, correcting and training in righteousness, so that the servant of God may be thoroughly equipped for every good work." Paul referred to *all* Scripture, which includes the unfulfilled prophecies of the Bible. These portions of God's Word are valuable for teaching what the future holds as well as standing against false teachings regarding what will occur in the end times.

Studying unfulfilled prophecy gives us hope. Romans 15:4 (NIV) teaches, "Everything that was written in the past was written to teach us, so that through the endurance taught in the Scriptures and the encouragement they provide we might have hope." When we understand God's plan for our future, we can live with hope even during our most difficult days. Prophecy is not intended to frighten those of us who believe but to encourage us. As 1 Thessalonians 4:18 (NIV) urges, "Encourage one another with these words."

Studying unfulfilled prophecy promotes holy living. "Since everything will be destroyed in this way, what kind of people ought you to be? You ought to live holy and godly lives as you look forward to the day of God and speed its coming" (2 Peter 3:11-12 NIV). A proper understanding of what the future holds directs our lives toward holiness now. Our goal is to live now in such a way that we have no regrets in the future when we stand before our Lord.

Studying unfulfilled prophecy compels us to share the gospel. When we understand that Christ's rapture could take place at any moment, "in a moment, in the twinkling of an eye" (1 Corinthians 15:52) according to the apostle Paul, we cannot help but long to share the reason for the hope within us (1 Peter 3:15).

Studying unfulfilled prophecy brings blessing. In Revelation 1:3 (NIV), John proclaims, "Blessed is the one who reads aloud the words of this prophecy, and blessed are those who hear it and take to heart what is written in it, because the time is near." In contrast, Revelation also teaches a curse upon those who add to the words of its prophecies or take away from them (Revelation 22:18-19).

Prophecy is worthy of our attention, study, and devotion. Paul wrote in 2 Timothy 2:15 (NIV), "Do your best to present yourself to God as one approved, a worker who does not need to be ashamed and who correctly handles the word of truth." This applies to our study of all Scripture, but it is certainly relevant to our understanding of the Bible's many prophecies. Our goal must be to know what God has spoken so that we may live with hope, holiness, and a desire to help those who have yet to experience a relationship with the risen Christ.

Jesus personally expected His followers to carefully study Scripture in preparation for His return. In Matthew 24:42 (NIV), He commanded His disciples, "Therefore keep watch, because you do not know on what day your Lord will come."

In contrast, Jesus condemned the religious leaders of His day because they did not recognize the signs of the times.

> The Pharisees and Sadducees came to Jesus and tested
> him by asking him to show them a sign from heaven.
> He replied, "When evening comes, you say, 'It will

be fair weather, for the sky is red,' and in the morning, 'Today it will be stormy, for the sky is red and overcast.' You know how to interpret the appearance of the sky, but you cannot interpret the signs of the times" (Matthew 16:1-3 NIV).

Jesus expected the people during His first coming to recognize Him and to eagerly anticipate His second coming. We are likewise called to both reflect on Christ's fulfillment of biblical prophecy and to look ahead at His future prophecies.

Biblical prophecies and their literal fulfillment fascinate our curiosity and challenge our minds, but they are ultimately intended to bring us to a personal point of decision and faith. If the Bible predicted these things would happen and they actually did happen, then we must take Jesus' claims about Himself seriously. If He alone fulfilled these prophecies, then He alone is the Savior, the Son of God, King of kings and Lord of lords. And if He is, then He deserves our faith, our lives, and our complete devotion.

Lesson 1

Only God Can Prophesy

When it comes to predicting the future, mankind has a poor record. We simply have no way of knowing what's going to happen tomorrow, next week, next month, or next year. By contrast, God knows the future and reveals glimpses of it in the Bible. And so far, every single prediction that's been fulfilled has occurred exactly the way God said it would. He has never even been slightly wrong.

1. Read Isaiah 46:9-10. What is God able to do that no one else can do?
2. Read Isaiah 45:5-7. What things does the Lord do? What does this tell you about Him?
3. Read Psalm 33:10-11. What does this passage say about the plans of people? What does it say about the plans of the Lord?
4. What does Proverbs 21:1 tell us about God?
5. Based on these Bible verses, how much control would you say God has over world events?
6. What does this knowledge do to your level of confidence in God's ability to fulfill all the predictions He made in the Bible?

─────

Applying Prophecy to Everyday Life

God is not only able to fulfill all the predictions in the Bible but also able to keep all His promises. How does that benefit you as a Christian?

UNDERSTANDING BIBLE PROPHECY

Finding your way through the maze of traffic in a major city can be difficult—especially if you don't know where you're going. Some people view Bible prophecy the same way. It looks like a hopeless maze of confusion about the future, so they throw up their hands in defeat. "I just can't make any sense out of this!" they exclaim in frustration.

One of the most difficult tasks in interpreting God's Word has been understanding the prophecies about the end times. First, we must remember that the people of Jesus' day missed many of the predictions of His first coming. Therefore, we must not presume that we have figured out all the details of His second coming. Second, we must guard against the great temptation to read prophecy through the eyes of the present. This has been a problem throughout church history. As early as the second century AD, believers have speculated about the time and place of the Lord's return.

Unfortunately, unguarded speculation has often prevailed as the most popular approach to biblical prophecy. Some of the wildest possible scenarios have received incredible popular support. In a few cases, prophecy has even been used by people to justify themselves and condemn their critics.

Yet prophecy is not so difficult to understand that it should be avoided. In fact, neglecting it could be dangerous to Christians' spiritual health. The apostle Paul obviously thought prophecy was important for young Christians to study, for he addressed it in every chapter in the little book of 1 Thessalonians, one of his earliest letters.

> Concerning the times and the seasons, brethren, you have no need that I should write to you. For you yourselves know perfectly that the day of the Lord so comes as a thief in the night. For when they say, "Peace and safety!" then sudden destruction comes upon them, as labor pains upon a pregnant woman. And they shall not escape. But you, brethren, are not in darkness, so that this Day should overtake you as a thief. You are all sons of light and sons of the day. We are not of the night nor of darkness (1 Thessalonians 5:1-5).

Clearly Paul did not think that "the day of the Lord" (a reference to the second coming of Christ) was too complex for these young believers. Some details of prophecy are complex, but the essentials are not.

In fact, even if some minor misunderstanding happens when studying Bible prophecy, this is still far better than ignoring the topic completely. Ignorance is not a blessing or virtue. Paul wrote, "I do not want you to be ignorant, brethren" (1 Thessalonians 4:13). Understanding God's plan for the future will motivate you to godly living now. Our goal must be to stand before the Lord on that final judgment day and hear the words, "Well done, good and faithful servant...Enter into the joy of your lord" (Matthew 25:23).

Why Christians Should Study Bible Prophecy

God has given three important signs that He is supernatural. First, He has given us creation. Second, He has revealed Himself to us through Jesus Christ. Third, He has provided written revelation concerning Himself in the Bible.

Creation provides clear evidence that God exists (Romans 1:19-20). It is impossible to find order in disorder. A growing body of scientific evidence supports a single origin of all space, time, and matter that is consistent with the biblical teaching of the eternal God as Creator of all things. All creation testifies that a God of creative design is behind this universe, including the earth and all people.

Jesus Christ is evidence of both God's existence and His unmatched love for all people. God sent His only Son Jesus into this world not only to identify with us but also to die on our behalf so God could forgive our sins and we could enjoy eternity with Him forever.

Yet the most detailed revelation available to us today is the Bible. Creation is limited; it cannot show us God's love or directions for living. Jesus is God in human form, yet His teachings depended on the Word of God. The written revelation in the Bible provides the information we need in order to know and obey His will. In fact, we would know very little about Christ if the Bible did not exist.

In the Bible we have an entire collection of truth that affirms the divine authorship and authority of Scripture in its fulfilled prophecies. Hundreds of predictions regarding Christ's first coming, including His birth, miracles, suffering, death, and resurrection, were foretold long before they occurred. In addition, we have been given numerous prophecies yet unfulfilled. Someone has counted eight times as many prophecies regarding Christ's second coming as for His first coming. This gives us great confidence that what has yet to take place will be fulfilled just as the prophecies related to Christ's first coming have been fulfilled.

The Bible provides many other reasons why we should study prophecy.

God evidently considers prophecy important, for He has included much of it in the Bible. Approximately one-third of the Bible's 66 inspired books were authored by prophets in the Old Testament. Even four of the New Testament's books—Revelation, 1 and 2 Thessalonians, and Jude—are primarily prophetic. In total, nearly one-fourth of all the verses in the Bible include prophecy. If we omit the study of prophecy because it is difficult or controversial, we will ignore an enormous portion of Scripture.

Prophecy reveals God's nature. Prophecy reveals the elevated status of Christ. At His second coming, Jesus will come "with power and great glory" (Matthew 24:30) as "King of kings and Lord of lords" (1 Timothy 6:15). Revelation 1:7 teaches, "every eye will see Him." Philippians 2:10-11 further reveals every knee will bow and every tongue will confess that Jesus Christ is Lord!

Prophecy guards against false and unhealthy teaching. Scripture provides an accurate understanding of both how to live today and what to expect in eternity. In contrast, groups such as Jehovah's Witnesses teach an afterlife that includes a special class of heaven for 144,000 people. This is based on an inaccurate view of Revelation 7:4-8. Mormon teachings describe three levels of the afterlife, contrary to the clear teachings of the Bible that teach only heaven or hell as the eternal resting place of the soul. A proper understanding of biblical teaching regarding what is to come provides help on these issues and others that shape our lives today.

Prophecy motivates evangelism. When we clearly see that Christ will return at any moment, we are motivated to share the gospel with those who have yet to believe in Him.

Prophecy also motivates holy living by believers. One tool the Holy Spirit uses to encourage Christians to live pure lives is the study of unfulfilled prophecy, especially where the Bible speaks of Christ's soon return. As 1 John 3:3 notes, "Everyone who has this hope in Him purifies himself, just as He is pure."

Prophecy offers hope in times of despair. We live in a world where much evil occurs. We may endure broken relationships, problems with our finances or careers, or other frustrations regarding the injustice or sin in the world around us. Yet Scripture confidently speaks of our future hope and eternal joy with Christ.

> Let not your heart be troubled; you believe in God, believe also in Me. In My Father's house are many mansions; if it were not so, I would have told you. I go to prepare a place for you. And if I go and prepare a place for you, I will come again and receive you to Myself; that where I am, there you may be also (John 14:1-3).

This great hope Christ gave to His disciples can inspire our lives still today. Only a study of the Bible's unfulfilled prophecies can change our hearts in all of these unique ways that help us honor God and bring glory to Him now and in eternity.

Prophetic Interpretation

We must understand not only the benefits of studying prophecy but also the keys to prophetic interpretation. Every imaginable speculation has arisen as to the identity of the Antichrist, the date of the rapture, and the beginning of the Battle of Armageddon. To make sense of all this, consider a simple paradigm.

Facts. Prophetic revelation includes clearly stated facts: Christ will return for His own, He will judge the world, there will be a time of great trouble on the earth at the end of the age, the final conflict will be won by Christ, and so on. These basic facts are clearly stated in Scripture.

Assumptions. Factual prophecy only tells us so much and no more. Beyond that we must make certain assumptions. If these are correct, they will lead to valid conclusions, but if not, they may lead to baseless speculations. For example, we may assume that Russia will invade Israel in the last days. Whether that is factual depends on the legitimacy of our interpretation of Ezekiel's Magog prophecy

(Ezekiel 38–39). To say we don't need to worry about Russia because it will be destroyed is foolish. That is only an assumption based upon one's interpretation of Magog's identity.

Speculations. These are purely calculated guesses based on assumptions. In many cases they have no basis in prophetic fact at all. For example, the Bible says the number of the Antichrist is 666 (Revelation 13:18). We can only speculate what this means. We may assume that it is a literal number that will appear on things in the last days. When one prominent evangelist saw the number 666 prefixed on automobile license plates in Israel a few years ago, he speculated that the "mark of the Beast" had already arrived in the Holy Land.

A Variety of Views

One of the challenges of understanding Bible prophecy is that people approach it with different methods of interpretation. Several approaches to eschatology, or the study of the last days, have arisen in the Christian church. Some people even refuse to consider prophecy at all, preferring to dismiss it as hopelessly confusing or generally irrelevant. But evangelical Christians have always taken prophecy seriously.

The issue at stake among evangelicals has generally been how a person interprets prophecy. Three main schools of thought have been proposed. Most evangelical Christians are premillennial, but some are amillennial or postmillennial.

Postmillennial. This school of thought asserts that the Millennium (the 1000-year reign of Christ mentioned in Revelation 20:1-3,6-7) is to be interpreted symbolically and is synonymous with the church age. Satan's power is viewed as being bound by the power of the gospel. Postmillennialists believe that during this Millennium (the church age), the church is called to conquer unbelief, convert the masses, and govern society by the mandate of biblical law. Only after Christianity succeeds on earth will Christ return and announce that His kingdom has been realized. Advocates of postmillennialism urge believers to take dominion over the earth and its political governments in order to usher in the kingdom of God on earth.

Those who hold to this perspective believe that the world will continue to get better and better until the entire world is Christianized, at which time Christ will return to a kingdom already flourishing in peace. Although this view was popular at the beginning of the twentieth century, it was all but eliminated as a result of the World Wars, the Great Depression, and the overwhelming escalation of moral evil in society. Many who previously held postmillennial views adopted the amillennial position. However, postmillennialism is currently gaining some resurgence. It continues to promote the entrance of the kingdom prior to the return of the King.

Amillennial. This approach sees no Millennium of any kind on the earth. Rather, amillennialists tend to view so-called millennial prophecies as being fulfilled in eternity. Biblical references to the thousand years are interpreted symbolically. In this scheme, the church age ends with the return of Christ to judge the world and usher in eternity. God's promises to Israel are viewed as having been fulfilled in the church (the New Israel of the new covenant); therefore, amillennialists see no specific future for national Israel. They view the church age as an era of conflict between the forces of good and evil that culminates with the return of Christ.

Amillennialists do not believe in a literal kingdom on the earth following the second coming of Christ. They tend to spiritualize and allegorize the prophecies concerning the Millennium and attribute yet-unfulfilled prophecies relating to Israel to the church instead. Those who hold to amillennialism also believe Satan was bound at Christ's first appearance on earth 2000 years ago. Furthermore, its adherents differ as to whether the Millennium is being spiritually fulfilled currently on earth or whether it's being fulfilled by the saints in heaven. However, they tend to agree that our current state of affairs is probably as good as it's going to get and that the eternal state (heaven), not the millennial kingdom, will immediately follow the second coming of Christ. Those who hold to this view do not adhere to a simple and plain literal interpretation of Scripture.

Premillennial. This view says that Christ will return at the end of the church age to set up His kingdom on earth for a literal 1000 years. Most premillennialists also believe there will be a period of great tribulation on earth prior to the return of Christ. Some premillennialists believe the church will go through the Tribulation (posttribulationists), others believe the church will be raptured prior to the Tribulation (pretribulationists), and a small number believe the church will be raptured in the middle of the Tribulation (midtribulationists). Despite these differences in regard to the rapture of the church, premillennialists generally believe in the future restoration of the state of Israel and the eventual conversion of the Jews to Christianity.

Most evangelical Christians hold to the dispensational premillennial view of eschatology, which looks forward to the rapture of believers to heaven as the next major prophetic event to be fulfilled. This, they believe, will end the church age and prepare the way for the Tribulation and the return of Christ. One Bible passage that suggests the rapture is 1 Thessalonians 4:16-17.

> The Lord Himself will descend from heaven with a shout, with the voice of an archangel, and with the trumpet call of God. And the dead in Christ will rise first. Then we who are alive and remain shall be caught up together with them in the clouds to meet the Lord in the air. And thus we shall always be with the Lord.

Early Christians were unquestionably premillennialists. The disciples and those they taught anticipated the return of Christ and the establishment of His kingdom on earth in their lifetime. Detractors of the premillennial view claim that it is relatively new theology. But scholars have demonstrated that premillennialism was the dominant view held during the first three centuries of the early church.

Premillennialists believe that the rapture, the Tribulation, and the glorious appearance of Christ will all occur before the beginning of the Millennium. During the Millennium, Satan will be bound for 1000 years, and a theocratic kingdom of peace will ensue with Jesus as its King. The righteous will have been raised from the dead prior to the Millennium and will participate in its blessings (Revelation 20:4).

Toward the end of the third century, an allegorical approach to Scripture began to dominate theological thought. Philosophy replaced the study of Scripture, and premillennialism fell into disrepute. Not until after the Reformation was there a revival of premillennial thought. Later, in the nineteenth century, Bible institutes and Christian schools across America began to emphasize a literal interpretation of the Bible, and with it, a return to premillennialism. Today, despite continued attacks, premillennialism is the dominant millennial view.

Taking Prophecy Seriously

Evangelical Christians take seriously the Bible's prophecies about such topics as the rapture, the Tribulation, Armageddon, and the return of Christ. In fact, many are convinced that the march to Armageddon, the last great battle, has already begun. They sense that the stage is being set, that we are living in the end times, and that the world will soon be plunged into a series of cataclysmic wars that may well claim three-fourths of the world's population.

In recent years, more and more of the secular community has come to agree that we seem to be approaching the end of the world. Nobel laureates and other reputable scientists have warned that the earth's time clock is running out. Air and water pollution, the evaporation of the protective ozone layer, the elimination of oxygen-producing

and the general instability of the earth's crust have all been
ous problems that could hinder the future of life on this
planet. The current proliferation of weapons of mass destruction is
almost beyond belief, and many of those weapons are suspected to be
in the hands of unscrupulous terrorists.

In past centuries, when Christians talked about the end of the
world, people often laughed at them because they could not con-
ceive of the entire planet being destroyed. But today, both Christians and skeptics realize that such destruction is well within the
realm of possibility.

The Bible warns us that the "day of the Lord so comes as a thief
in the night" (1 Thessalonians 5:2). It will be an instantaneous event
that will catch the world unprepared. In fact, the Bible reminds us
that people will promise, "'Peace, peace!' when there is no peace"
(Jeremiah 8:11; see also Ezekiel 13:10).

People have consistently demonstrated that they cannot bring
a permanent and lasting peace to this world. Every human effort
at peace has been short-lived and destined to failure. At the end of
time, when the stakes are the highest, the greatest gamble ever made
for peace will end in the greatest battle of all time—at Armageddon.

Interpreting the Bible Literally

One of the most important keys to studying Bible prophecy is
to interpret the text literally. One of the basic rules of biblical interpretation is this: If the literal sense makes good sense, seek no other
sense, lest it result in nonsense. When evangelical Christians read
the Bible, we take literally its statements about Jesus' birth in Bethlehem, His ministry in Galilee, and His miracles of healing the sick
and raising the dead. We believe He was literally crucified and bur-
ied and that He literally rose from the dead. So why shouldn't we
believe He will literally come back one day?

We understand, of course, that the Bible sometimes uses figurative language. For example, Jesus is called the Lamb of God 28 times in the book of Revelation. This does not mean that He is a literal lamb. The term "Lamb," in reference to Christ, is intended to give us a symbolic picture of Christ as our atoning sacrifice. But the symbolic use of "Lamb" does not eliminate the literal truth of Christ as our atoning sacrifice.

Prophecy scholar Paul N. Benware provides us with some very important additional principles to help us interpret prophecy literally.

Interpret by comparing prophecy with prophecy. Prophecies weave their way from some of the earliest chapters in Genesis to the very end of Revelation. Thus, the interpreter of prophecy should compare Scripture with Scripture in order to ascertain the entire teaching on prophetic subjects. By so doing, a complete and accurate picture comes into focus of what God is going to do and perhaps how and why He is going to do it.

Interpret in light of possible time intervals. Because the ancients did not fully understand the flow of time, sometimes the prophetic message compresses the time between events. This telescoping phenomenon is common in the prophets and reveals gaps in prophetic fulfillment. A key passage to illustrate this is Daniel 9:24-27, where such a gap is critical in properly understanding the prophecy. Of course, only in the progress of God's revelation can we see such intervals of time between prophetic fulfillments.[1]

The prophecies of Christ's first coming were fulfilled literally in minute detail. Therefore, we have every confidence that the prophecies of His second coming will be fulfilled literally as well. Jesus really is coming back to rapture believers and take them to the Father's house (John 14:1-3). He is also coming again to judge the world, defeat the Antichrist, bind Satan, and bring the kingdom of heaven to earth. That leaves us with only one question: When?

Understanding Bible Prophecy

Too often, Christians have been reluctant to study Bible prophecy because they fear it's too complicated or controversial. But if God included literally hundreds of prophecies in the Bible, surely He did so for a reason! He wants us to know what the future holds. He wants us to recognize that He is fully in control, that Christ will rule the world someday, and that we have a wonderful eternity to look forward to. If you are a Christian, the more you understand Bible prophecy, the more you will enjoy the confidence and security that come from knowing that nothing will change the final outcome that God has determined.

1. The Old Testament contains many prophecies that predict the first coming of Christ and His gift of salvation. According to 1 Peter 1:10, what attitude did the Old Testament prophets have toward these prophecies?

2. Read 1 Peter 1:12. Who were the Old Testament prophets ministering to when they proclaimed their prophecies?

3. And what did the "angels desire to look into"?

4. Virtually the entire book of Revelation is prophetic. What benefit does Revelation 1:3 say will be experienced by "those who hear the words of this prophecy"?

5. We can see, then, that a right attitude toward prophecy is important. In addition, what does Titus 2:12 say about how we should live "in the present age"?

6. What are we to look for, according to Titus 2:13?

Applying Prophecy to Everyday Life

How is God helping you to better appreciate the importance of Bible prophecy and what it means to your daily life?

3

ARE WE LIVING IN THE LAST DAYS?

The apostle Paul looked down the corridor of time into the distant future and predicted, "In the last days perilous times will come" (2 Timothy 3:1). Are those days here now? Is the coming of Christ on the horizon?

The world is changing every day. We are standing on the edge of a new day in world politics. The dramatic changes we have witnessed in Europe, the Middle East, and the former Soviet Union tell us that the world is undergoing a massive transformation. The aftermath of World War II has long since been shaken from us like dust from an old rag. Eastern Europe is awakening to a new day of hope and freedom. But turmoil in the Middle East reminds us that the world is still facing difficult days ahead.

At the same time, there is great concern about where all these changes are taking us. Charles Colson has said, "We sense that things are winding down, that somehow freedom, justice, and order are slipping away. Our great civilization may not yet lie in smoldering ruins, but the enemy is within the gates. The times seem to smell of sunset."[1] He goes on to suggest that Western civilization is facing the greatest crisis encountered since the barbarians invaded Rome.

Many believe we have now moved to the final round in the struggle for world dominion. The collapse of communism removed one of the significant players in what one writer called the "Millennial Endgame." But the end of the Cold War is by no means the end of the struggle for world supremacy.

Our neglect of God's revelation has pushed us to the limits of our own rationalization. We have abandoned rationality for irrationality in the attempt to hold onto belief in something—anything—beyond ourselves. All through the twentieth century, we allowed godless secularism to replace the Judeo-Christian values of our society. We deliberately and systematically removed God from prominence in our culture and in our intellectual lives. We have made Him irrelevant to our culture.

Tragically, we have also made our culture irrelevant to God. In so doing, we have abandoned our spiritual heritage. The Christian consensus that once dominated Western culture is now shattered. The world is already mired in the quicksand of secularism, relativism, and mysticism. In the place of biblical Christianity, people are now calling for the New World Order, which consists of the very elements Scripture warns will signify the empire of the Antichrist.

World government. Globalists are now insisting that national governments should surrender their sovereignty to a one-world government. Such a government would operate through a world headquarters, a world court, and even a world military. Today, many serious voices are calling for such a reality.

World economy. The rampant spread of globalism is fueled by the driving force of the world economy. It is virtually impossible to do business today without networking with the global economy. There is almost no such thing as an American product that is not dependent on parts, trade, or investments from foreign countries.

World religion. This will be the final phase of the New World Order. The idea of a new world religion of peace and cooperation is already being proposed. Religious unity has been endorsed by Catholic popes, the Dalai Lama, and leaders of the World Council of Churches.

What we are witnessing today may well be the fulfillment of the biblical prophecies of the end times. Revelation 13 predicts the rise of a powerful world ruler who is able to control the world politically and economically. This ruler will have at his side a false prophet who promotes a one-world religion.

The New World Order

The economic unification of the European Union brought a new wave of optimism to Europe. The Europe of the future may well be a political union, the United States of Europe. If this happens, Europe, not America, will be the strongest and most powerful "nation" on earth—economically, politically, and even militarily. And if the current European Union were to eventually include the former Soviet satellites of Eastern Europe and even Russia itself, Europe would stretch from the Atlantic Ocean to the Pacific Ocean for the first time in history!

The key players in the New Europe will be England, France, Germany, and Russia. The unification or cooperation of these four superstates could well determine the issue of who controls the world of the future.

Many Christians believe that the New Europe fulfills the biblical prophecies of a revived Roman Empire in the last days. Like the architects of the Tower of Babel, advocates of the New World Order believe that "coming together" will consolidate formerly volatile or weak economies and foster global peace and cooperation. Helmut Kohl has said, "The United States of Europe will form the core of a peaceful order...the age prophesied of old, when all shall dwell secure and none shall make them afraid."[2]

The real tragedy in all this talk of global unity is the absence of any emphasis on the spiritual roots of democracy and freedom. The gospel has been blunted in Western Europe for so long that there is little God-consciousness left in the European people. Without Christ, the Prince of Peace, there can be no hope for man-made orders of peace and prosperity. There will be no Millennium without the Messiah!

Where Are We Now?

We can now see more clearly than ever that we have taken a quantum leap toward the fulfillment of the biblical prophecies of the last days. The stage is set for the climactic act in the long history of the human drama and for the fulfillment of the prophecies of the end times.

1. The fall of communism has paved the way for a world economy and a world government. The global web is tightening around us every day.

2. Secularism is giving way to New Age mysticism as the do-it-yourself religion of our times. The end result will be the watering down of religious beliefs so that they are more palatable to the general public.

3. Global economic interdependence will eventually lead to a global political system that trumps national sovereignty.

4. Materialism and preoccupation with self is replacing spiritual values. Mankind is mindlessly pursuing material prosperity as the basis for meaning and value in life.

5. The spiritual vacuum that results will leave the world ready for the ultimate deception: the great lie of the Antichrist, which will deceive the whole world.

6. This world leader will quickly arise on the international scene, promising to bring peace and economic stability. He will receive the support of the European community and eventually control the whole world.

7. A crisis in the Middle East will trigger this world leader's intervention militarily and politically. He will eventually sign a peace treaty with Israel, only to break it later.

8. A false prophet of international fame will suddenly emerge to gain control of the world religious system and use it to reinforce the worship of Antichrist.

9. Resistance to the world system will be crushed by a massive worldwide persecution. Men, women, and children will be slaughtered in the name of the world state.

10. Israel will become the central figure in the conflict with the world state. The Antichrist will eventually break his covenant with Israel and invade it, setting the stage for the Battle of Armageddon.

How Certain Is Christ's Second Coming?

The failed predictions by certain modern prophets of Christ's return on a certain date have caused many to mock or question whether the Lord will return at all. All too often people overreact to man's failed predictions and reject prophecy altogether. Unfortunately, this often leads to them overlooking the clear statements in the Bible about Christ's return. How certain is Christ's second coming?

The Lord's second coming is mentioned eight times more frequently in the Old Testament and New Testament than His first coming. In fact, Christ's second coming is evidently the second-most important doctrine in the entire New Testament, for the only teaching mentioned more frequently is the subject of salvation! His coming is mentioned 318 times in the 260 chapters of the New Testament alone. All nine authors of the New Testament mentioned it.

Christ's second coming is mentioned or alluded to in twenty-three of the twenty-seven New Testament books, and of the four books that make no clear mention of it, three (Philemon, 2 John, and 3 John) are one-chapter personal letters. Only one doctrinal book makes no specific mention of the subject (Galatians), although an implied reference to the events appears in 1:4.

To help you appreciate the New Testament's emphasis on the coming of Christ, let's take a quick look at its books one at a time.

Matthew. Two entire chapters, 24 and 25, are devoted to this subject. Often called the Olivet Discourse, this message was delivered just prior to our Lord's death. This sermon contains the most important and complete chronology of future events found in Scripture with the exception of the book of Revelation.

Mark. Mark devotes chapter 13 to the Olivet Discourse prophecies of the end times, culminating in the second coming of Christ.

Luke. This great first-century historian and doctor included the second-coming prophecies in chapters 17 and 21 of this book. He wrote, "Then they will see the Son of Man coming in a cloud with power and great glory" (21:27).

John. The "beloved disciple" who outlived all the other apostles wrote his life of Christ about 50 years after Christ ascended into heaven. Although he does not repeat the Olivet Discourse as do the other three Gospel writers, he quotes one of the clearest promises to come from the Savior's lips on this subject.

> Let not your heart be troubled; you believe in God, believe also in Me. In My Father's house are many mansions; if it were not so, I would have told you. I go to prepare a place for you. And if I go and prepare a place for you, I will come again and receive you to Myself; that where I am, there you may be also (14:1-3).

Acts. Luke's excellent record of the work of the Holy Spirit through the lives of the apostles contains several promises of Christ's second coming. The first act of the ascended Christ was to dispatch two angelic messengers to make this announcement to His disciples: "Men of Galilee, why do you stand gazing up into heaven? This same Jesus, who was taken up from you into heaven, will so come in like manner as you saw Him go into heaven" (1:11).

In addition, the first sermon Peter preached after the day of Pentecost records this promise given to the Jews of Jerusalem, many of whom had doubtless called for the death of Christ: "Repent therefore and be converted, that your sins may be blotted out, so that times of refreshing may come from the presence of the Lord, and that He may send Jesus Christ, who was preached to you before" (3:19-20). The acts of the first-century apostles were motivated by both the Holy Spirit and the expectation of Jesus' return to this earth.

The thirteen epistles of Paul. The writings of the apostle Paul had a tremendous impact on the early church. Paul imparted deep doctrinal teaching, practical exhortation, correction, and instruction on many aspects of the Christian life. Thirteen times he mentioned baptism, and only twice did he touch on communion, yet he mentioned the second coming of our Lord 50 times.

First Thessalonians is considered the first letter Paul wrote. In it he referred the young believers at Thessalonica to the second coming of Christ in every chapter! (See 1:10; 2:19; 3:13; 4:13-18; 5:2,23.) He repeated that emphasis in even greater detail in 2 Thessalonians (see 1:7-10; 2:1-12; 3:5). These epistles demonstrate how soon and how insistently Paul taught new converts the doctrine of Christ's return, for he was in their city only three weeks before angry Jews drove him out of town.

We also see the apostle's love of the second coming in his rather stern words at the conclusion of 1 Corinthians: "If anyone does not love the Lord Jesus Christ, let him be accursed. O Lord, come!" (16:22). The Greek word Paul used in that last phrase, *maranatha,* means "the Lord is coming." That expression gained popularity in the first century and became a common mode of greeting and parting. Christians often included it in letters, and in some cases even soldiers used it as a slogan when they went off to war.

All but two of Paul's epistles refer to the second coming. He alluded to it obliquely in Romans 11:26 and in 14:10, where he talks about the judgment seat of Christ. That judgment is described in detail in 1 Corinthians 3:9-15. Then in 1 Corinthians 15 Paul describes the resurrection of the body (verses 35-49) and gives details of the rapture (verses 50-58). He also refers to some of these same second-coming truths in 2 Corinthians 1:14 and 5:10. Galatians, which offers a deep discussion on the finished work of Christ on the cross, does not contain a clear reference to the second coming, though an allusion to the event appears in 1:4. Ephesians presents the Christian "in the heavenly places," and "the day of redemption" (1:3; 4:30) can only mean the day of deliverance through Christ's return. Philippians contains several references to the Lord's coming, the best of which is Philippians 3:20-21:

> Our citizenship is in heaven, from which we also eagerly wait for the Savior, the Lord Jesus Christ, who will transform our lowly body that it may be conformed to His glorious body, according to the working by which He is able even to subdue all things to Himself.

A thrilling promise appears in Colossians: "When Christ who is our life appears, then you will also appear with Him in glory" (3:4).

Like 1 and 2 Thessalonians, the epistles to Timothy provide many references to the second coming of Christ. Second Timothy 1:10 and 4:1,8 refer to "the appearing" and "His appearing."

In the book of Titus, a veteran servant of God advises a young preacher on how to conduct the work of the Lord in the church. Paul challenges Titus to teach people to deny themselves "ungodliness and worldly lusts…[to] live soberly, righteously, and godly in the present age, looking for the blessed hope and glorious appearing of our Great God and Savior Jesus Christ" (2:12-13).

When all the books of Paul are considered, we find that only two of thirteen omit mention of the second coming, and one of these is Philemon, a personal letter of only one chapter. There is no question the apostle Paul was absolutely certain that his Lord and Savior was coming back to this earth again.

Hebrews. This is a magnificent presentation of Christ as the fulfillment of the Old Testament types and symbols. It promises our Lord's return: "Christ was offered once to bear the sins of many. To those who eagerly wait for Him He will appear a second time, apart from sin, for salvation" (9:28).

James. This little book, which challenges Christians to show their faith by their works, culminates with a strong appeal relative to the coming of Christ: "Be patient. Establish your hearts, for the coming of the Lord is at hand" (5:8).

Peter. Writing to believers who were undergoing the trials of persecution, the apostle Peter challenged the elders to be faithful leaders on the basis of the Lord's coming: "When the Chief Shepherd appears, you will receive the crown of glory that does not fade away" (1 Peter 5:4). Peter's second epistle contains a lengthy prophecy concerning the rise of scoffers in the days just preceding Christ's coming. He promises that in spite of their ridicule, "the day of the Lord will come as a thief in the night" (2 Peter 3:10).

First John. The beautiful epistle that brings us assurance of salvation and confidence also challenges us to holy living on the basis of Christ's second coming. Here's an example: "Now, little children, abide in Him, that when He appears, we may have confidence and not be ashamed before Him at His coming" (2:28).

Jude. This tiny, one-chapter book contains a quotation from the patriarch Enoch, who walked in intimate fellowship with God during the chaotic days preceding the flood and who suddenly went directly to be with God. Genesis 5:24 says, "And Enoch walked with God; and he was not, for God took him." Some prophecy teachers suggest that Enoch's experience is symbolic of what will happen to Christians just before the chaotic days of the Tribulation, when the Lord will suddenly take Christians off this earth to be with Himself (see 1 Thessalonians 4:13-18 and 1 Corinthians 15:51-52).

Revelation. The Bible ends with an entire book filled with prophecies about the second coming. It directs us to a study of things forecast from the first century after Christ's ascension all the way until the end of the world.

Although we've just listed many of the outstanding references to the Lord's coming from Matthew to Revelation, this list is by no means exhaustive. There is much more material God has provided in His Word to establish the absolute certainty of His Son's coming back to this earth.

How Close Are We to the End?

We are undoubtedly fast approaching the final chapter of human history. The hoofbeats of the four horsemen of the Apocalypse can now be heard in the distance. The stage is set for the final act of human drama. The clock is ticking away the last seconds of any hope for a reprieve. We are being swept down the corridor of time to an inevitable date with destiny.

How much time is left? Only God knows. We must use every means at our disposal to preach the gospel of God's saving grace everywhere we can while we still have time. This is not the time to rest on our laurels. Rather, we have a window of opportunity, by the grace of God, and we need to take advantage of it right now. It is time for us to take seriously our responsibility to evangelize the world in our lifetime.

If we do not meet this challenge and fulfill our obligation, every kind of false religious cult, every kind of secular materialism, and every kind of moral perversion will rush to fill the vacuum. We alone have the truth that can set the world free from spiritual oppression. We must be willing to do all we can to fill that void—now!

Jesus Christ said what we all must realize at this crucial hour: "As long as it is day, we must do the work of him who sent me. Night is coming, when no one can work" (John 9:4 NIV). To the ancient church at Philadelphia, our Lord said, "I have set before you an open door, and no one can shut it" (Revelation 3:8). God has also given today's church an open door to preach the gospel where it has not yet been heard. May we rise to the occasion, recognizing that the ultimate struggle for world dominion is between the forces of Christ and the forces of evil.

Are We Living in the Last Days?

We twenty-first-century Christians live in exciting times. We don't know exactly when Christ will return, but we do know that His coming is drawing closer and closer. The evidence around us indicates more and more that we live in the very kind of society the Bible warned would arise in the days before the second coming. It's fascinating to watch history unfold as Scripture's description of the last days becomes reality before our very eyes.

1. Read John 14:1-3. What does verse 2 say Jesus is doing right now? What promise does Jesus give in verse 3?

2. Jesus talked about the destruction of the Temple in Matthew 24:1-2. What two questions did the disciples ask in response (see verse 3)?

3. What was Jesus' ultimate answer to the disciples (see verse 36)?

4. We cannot predict when Jesus will return, so some Christians decide that studying the times is not important. But what exhortation are we given in Ephesians 5:15-16? Why?

5. What will people be like in the last days, according to 2 Timothy 3:1-5? How many of these characteristics do you see manifest in our world today?

6. What additional problems will arise in the last days, according to 2 Timothy 4:2-4?

7. How are we to respond to these problems (see 2 Timothy 4:2,5)?

Applying Prophecy to Everyday Life

Read 2 Timothy 2:15. Are you able to handle "the word of truth" well enough to do your part in defending against wrong teaching and wrong living? What improvements would you like to make?

THE RAPTURE OF THE CHURCH

O ne of the most compelling and exciting prophetic events described in the Bible is the rapture of the church. It is clearly taught in 1 Thessalonians 4:15-18, where the apostle Paul provides us with these details:

> This we say to you by the word of the Lord, that we who are alive and remain until the coming of the Lord will by no means precede those who are asleep. For the Lord Himself will descend from heaven with a shout, with the voice of an archangel, and with the trumpet of God. And the dead in Christ will rise first. Then we who are alive and remain shall be caught up together with them in the clouds to meet the Lord in the air. And thus we shall always be with the Lord. Therefore comfort one another with these words.

This passage of Scripture mentions five stages to the rapture.

1. The Lord Himself will descend from heaven with a shout and with the sound of a trumpet.

2. The dead in Christ will rise first.

3. Then we who are alive and remain on the earth will be caught up together with them in the clouds.

4. We will meet the Lord in the air.

5. And we will always be with Him.

The English word "rapture" comes from the Latin *rapto*, which is a translation of the Greek New Testament word *harpazo*. All these terms mean "caught up" or "snatched away." The word "rapture" does not appear in English translations, but the concept of the rapture certainly does.

The Mystery of the Rapture

The apostle Paul also unveiled what he referred to as a mystery pertaining to the rapture. He explained that some Christians will never sleep (die). Instead, their bodies will be instantly transformed.

> Behold, I tell you a mystery: We shall not all sleep, but we shall all be changed—in a moment, in the twinkling of an eye, at the last trumpet. For the trumpet will sound, and the dead will be raised incorruptible, and we shall be changed. For this corruptible must put on incorruption, and this mortal must put on immortality (1 Corinthians 15:51-53).

Without warning, at the moment of the rapture, the bodies of all believers who have died since the day of Pentecost will suddenly be transformed into new, living, immortal, resurrected bodies. Even those whose bodies have long since decayed or whose ashes have been scattered across the oceans will receive new bodies. These new bodies will be joined together with the people's spirits, which Jesus brings with Him from heaven. Then the bodies of those who are alive on earth and have accepted Christ as their Savior will also be instantly translated into new, immortal bodies.

Paul provides similar descriptions of the rapture in 1 Corinthians 15:51-53 and 1 Thessalonians 4:15-18. When Christ comes to take His church (all believers) to heaven in fulfillment of His promise in John 14:1-3, He will include all New Testament believers, both the living and the dead.

Together, all believers will be instantaneously transported into the heavens to meet first their loved ones "in the clouds" and then to meet the Lord in the air. Those who have rejected the salvation of Jesus Christ and remain on earth will witness a miraculous event of astonishing proportions—the sudden mass disappearance of millions upon millions of Christians.

The rapture is often referred to as "the blessed hope" (Titus 2:13) because it provides comfort to believers who are concerned about the coming Tribulation and to those who long to be reunited with their departed loved ones who share faith in Christ.

The second coming, which encompasses both the rapture and the glorious appearing, is one of the most significant events mentioned in the entire Bible. There are 318 references in the New Testament alone of this awesome event, making it the second-most prominent doctrine presented in Scripture after salvation.

The doctrine of the second coming is clearly taught in both the Old and New Testaments. It is also affirmed in the doctrinal statement of every major Christian denomination. On average, the New Testament mentions the second coming in one out of every 30 verses, and it is mentioned in every chapter of 1 and 2 Thessalonians, the first books written for the early church. Moreover, all nine New Testament authors mention the second coming, and 23 of the 27 New Testament books reference it. Obviously God intended His church to be motivated to holiness, evangelism, and missionary concern by the study of the second coming of Christ.

Jesus' Most Direct Reference to the Rapture

Our Lord obviously referred to the rapture in John 14:1-3. All His other teachings on His return have to do with the second phase, or His literal, physical return, after which He will set up the kingdom, which His Jewish listeners anticipated. However, the day before Jesus died on the cross, He spoke these comforting words to His disciples to sustain them during His absence (the church age):

> Let not your heart be troubled; you believe in God, believe also in Me. In My Father's house are many mansions; if it were not so, I would have told you. I go to prepare a place for you. And if I go and prepare a place for you, I will come again and receive you to Myself; that where I am, there you may be also.

What did Jesus have in mind? He clearly spoke of a place He would travel to—His Father's house. Second, His Father's house includes many mansions (or "rooms" in some translations). The Father's house will have ample space for all of His children. Third, Jesus was leaving to prepare the place where He would take His followers. Fourth, Jesus promised to return to take His followers to be with Him. Finally, they would dwell together, forever, in the Father's house. Jesus clearly taught He would return for His followers to take them to the Father's house.

Two Phases of the Second Coming

The biblical references to the second coming clearly describe two distinct phases. There are simply too many conflicting elements in these phases to merge them into a single event. In the first phase, Jesus will come suddenly to rapture His church in the air and take all believers to His Father's house in fulfillment of His promise in John 14:1-3. There, they will appear before the judgment seat of Christ (2 Corinthians 5:9-10) and participate in the marriage supper of the Lamb (Revelation 19:1-10).

During this time, those left behind on the earth will experience the trials of the horrendous seven-year Tribulation period. Then Jesus will conclude the Tribulation with the second phase of His second coming by returning to earth in great power and glory to stop the slaughter and set up His millennial kingdom. So the entire second coming could be compared to a two-act play (the rapture and the glorious appearance) separated by a seven-year intermission (the Tribulation). The apostle Paul distinguishes between these two phases in Titus 2:13, where he refers to the rapture as the "blessed hope" and the return of Christ to the earth as the "glorious appearing."

Some theologians attempt to dismiss the multiphase aspect of Christ's second coming. They place both the rapture and the glorious appearing at the end of the Tribulation (the posttribulation view of the rapture). In this scenario, Christians will be required to face the horrors of the Tribulation.

In order to hold this view, one must either spiritualize away or simply ignore numerous passages of Scripture. A careful study of the many biblical references to the second coming clearly shows that the rapture and the glorious appearing are two separate phases of the second coming.

The Rapture of the Church	The Glorious Appearing
1. Christ comes for believers in the air.	1. Christ comes with believers to the earth.
2. All Christians on earth are translated into new bodies.	2. There is no translation of bodies.

The Rapture of the Church	The Glorious Appearing
3. Christians are taken to the Father's house in heaven.	3. Resurrected saints remain on the earth.
4. There is no judgment on the earth.	4. Christ judges the inhabitants of the earth.
5. The church will be taken to heaven.	5. Christ sets up His kingdom on earth.
6. It could occur at any time (it is imminent).	6. It cannot occur until the end of the seven-year Tribulation period.
7. There are no signs preceding it.	7. There are numerous signs preceding it.
8. It affects only believers.	8. It affects all humanity.
9. It is a time of joy.	9. It is a time of mourning.
10. It occurs before the "day of wrath."	10. It occurs after the "day of wrath."
11. Satan is not bound, but wreaks havoc on the earth.	11 Satan is bound in the abyss for 1000 years.
12. Christians are judged at the judgment seat of Christ.	12. Christians have already been judged at the judgment seat.
13. The marriage of the Lamb takes place.	13. The marriage of the Lamb has already taken place.
14. Only Christ's own will see Him.	14. All those on earth will see Him.
15. The seven-year Tribulation follows.	15. The 1000-year Millennium follows.

As we have seen, various views exist as to when the rapture will occur (before, during, or after the Tribulation), but surely there will be a rapture. The only real question is, when will it occur? Christ must return at some point to resurrect the dead in Christ and rapture the living believers in order to take us all to the Father's house in heaven, as He promised in John 14:1-4. There are a number of reasons to believe the rapture will occur before the Tribulation begins.

The Lord Himself promised to deliver us. Revelation 3:10 says, "Because you have kept My command to persevere, I also will keep you from the hour of trial which shall come upon the whole world, to test those who dwell on the earth." The Greek word *ek*, which literally means "out of," is translated in this passage as "from." In other words, it is the Lord's intention to keep the church out of the Tribulation. Therefore, the rapture must occur before the Tribulation begins.

The church is to be delivered from the wrath to come. The apostle Paul tells us in 1 Thessalonians 1:10 that we should "wait for His Son from heaven, whom He raised from the dead, even Jesus who delivers us from the wrath to come." The context of this particular passage is the rapture. The church must therefore be removed from the earth before the Tribulation begins in order to be delivered from the wrath to come.

The church is not appointed to wrath. According to 1 Thessalonians 5:9, "God did not appoint us to wrath, but to obtain salvation through our Lord Jesus Christ." Once again, the context of this passage is the rapture. The Tribulation is prophesied as a time of God's wrath, and Christians are not appointed to wrath, so it follows that the church must be raptured out of the way before the Tribulation begins.

The church is absent from Revelation 4–18. Revelation 4–18 details the events of the Tribulation. The church is mentioned 17 times in the first three chapters of Revelation, but after John (who is a member of the church) is taken up to heaven at the beginning of chapter 4, the church is not mentioned or seen again until chapter 19, when it appears at the marriage with Christ in heaven and then returns to earth with Jesus at His glorious appearing. Why is it missing from those chapters? Because the church isn't in the Tribulation. It will be raptured before it begins.

If the church is raptured at the end of the Tribulation, there will be no one left to repopulate the earth during the Millennium. Just before the Millennium begins, all those who survive the Tribulation but reject Jesus Christ as Savior will be cast into hell (Matthew 25:46). If the rapture occurred at the end of the Tribulation, as some believe it will, all Christians would be taken from the earth as well, leaving no one on earth with a natural body to repopulate the planet during the Millennium. We know from numerous Old Testament passages and Revelation 20:7-10 that there will be a huge population explosion during the Millennium. Where do these people come from? The answer is that those who miss the rapture and become believers during the Tribulation (thanks to the preaching of the 144,000 Jews and the two witnesses) and survive to the end will repopulate the earth. Large numbers of believers will be martyred during the Tribulation, but some will survive. These people will not be raptured at the end of the Tribulation in some sort of posttribulational rapture. Rather, they will enter Christ's millennial kingdom with their natural bodies to populate that kingdom. In order for this to be possible, the rapture must take place prior to the Tribulation instead of at the end of it.

One of the chief characteristics of the rapture is that it will be sudden and will catch people by surprise. "Of that day and hour no one knows" (Matthew 24:36), which is why Jesus warns us, "Be ready, for the Son of Man is coming at an hour when you do not expect" (Matthew 24:44). Only a pretribulation rapture preserves the expectation of His coming at any moment. Indeed, the rapture has appeared imminent to Christians of every generation throughout the ages. Nothing could better motivate us to holy living and fervent evangelism than to recognize that Jesus could come today. And one day He will! The trumpet will sound, the archangel will shout, and we will all go home to be with Jesus.

The Chronology of the Rapture

If we assemble New Testament references to the rapture in chronological order, this is what we find.

1. The Lord Himself will descend from His Father's house, where He is preparing a place for us (John 14:1-3; 1 Thessalonians 4:16).

2. He will receive us to Himself (John 14:1-3).

3. He will bring deceased believers with Him (1 Thessalonians 4:14-15).

4. The Lord will shout as He descends (1 Thessalonians 4:16). All this takes place in the "twinkling of an eye" (1 Corinthians 15:52).

5. We will hear the voice of the archangel (1 Thessalonians 4:16).

6. We will also hear the trumpet call of God (1 Thessalonians 4:16). Don't confuse this with the seventh trumpet of judgment on the world during the Tribulation in Revelation 11:15.

7. The dead in Christ will rise first. The corruptible ashes of their dead bodies will be made incorruptible and be joined together with their spirits (1 Thessalonians 4:16-17).

8. Then we who are alive and remain will be changed. Our corruptible bodies will be made immortal (1 Corinthians 15:51,53).

9. We will be caught up (raptured) together (1 Thessalonians 4:17).

10. Dead and living believers will have a monumental reunion with the Lord in the clouds (1 Thessalonians 4:17).

11. Christ will receive us to Himself and take us to the Father's house to be with Him (John 14:3).

12. "And thus we shall always be with the Lord" (1 Thessalonians 4:17).

13. We will stand before the judgment seat of Christ (Romans 14:10; 1 Corinthians 3:11-15; 2 Corinthians 5:10).

14. We will participate in the marriage supper of the Lamb (Revelation 19:9).

15. In the meantime, after the church is raptured, the world will suffer the unprecedented outpouring of God's wrath, which our Lord described as "great tribulation" (Matthew 24:21).

The Rapture of the Church

A careful look at the Bible shows that there are no more prophecies that must be fulfilled in order for the rapture to occur. In other words, the rapture—the moment in which Christ will take all New Testament believers up to heaven prior to the seven-year Tribulation—is the very next event that will take place on God's prophetic calendar. We know it will happen; we just don't know when.

1. Write here the five stages of the rapture as described in 1 Thessalonians 4:15-18 and in the list on page 50:

   1.

   2.

   3.

   4.

   5.

2. List here the five reasons for believing in a pretribulation rapture and the supporting verse references as given on pages 55-56:

   1.

   2.

3.

4.

5.

3. What specific action does Jesus say we're to take in regard to the rapture, according to Mark 13:32-33?
4. Read 1 John 2:28. What are we told to do in order to be ready for the coming of Christ?

―――∞∞∞―――

Applying Prophecy to Everyday Life

Why is it so important for us to live as though Christ could come at any moment? Try to come up with at least two or three reasons.

THE BELIEVER'S REWARDS

For the Bible-believing Christian, the second coming of Christ is one of the most eagerly anticipated events prophesied in the Bible. It's hard not to get excited!

> The Lord Himself will descend from heaven with a shout, with the voice of an archangel, and with the trumpet of God. And the dead in Christ will rise first. Then we who are alive and remain shall be caught up together with them in the clouds to meet the Lord in the air. And thus we shall always be with the Lord (1 Thessalonians 4:16-17).

We all have friends and loved ones who have passed on and with whom we long to be reunited. As ecstatic as that experience will be, it will be eclipsed by our first meeting with the very Lord who died for us, forgave us, saved us, guided us through life, and resurrected us. Words will not be able to adequately express the joy of that moment.

What tends to get overlooked in all this is that immediately following the rapture, we will stand before the judgment seat of Christ and give an account of our actions while on earth.

Christ Will Be Our Judge

First Corinthians 4:5 tells us to "judge nothing before the time, until the Lord comes, who will both bring to light the hidden things of darkness and reveal the counsels of the hearts." This clearly says that the Lord will judge us at His coming. Many Christians have been lulled into a false state of complacency regarding this judgment. Some think there is no call on their lives to serve the Lord. Consequently, they accept His salvation as a gift and do nothing to advance His kingdom. If Christians truly understood the eternal significance of good works, they would radically alter their lifestyle.

> By grace you have been saved through faith, and that not of yourselves; it is the gift of God, not of works, lest anyone should boast. For we are His workmanship, created in Christ Jesus for good works, which God prepared beforehand that we should walk in them (Ephesians 2:8-10).

Although we are indeed saved by grace and not by our works, the Lord still expects us to do good works for Him once we are saved. In fact, we will be rewarded in the life to come in direct proportion to the way in which we have served Him. "We must all appear before the judgment seat of Christ, that each one may receive the things done in the body, according to what he has done, whether good or bad" (2 Corinthians 5:10).

The Judgment Seat of Christ

This judgment of our works will determine our position of service during the Millennium and may affect our status in heaven throughout eternity. This judgment of believers, which takes place at the judgment seat (Greek, *bema*) of Christ in heaven following the rapture, is a time of reward and is not to be confused with the Great White Throne Judgment of unbelievers (Revelation 20:11-15). The apostle Paul describes the bema seat judgment of believers:

> No other foundation can anyone lay than that which is laid, which is Jesus Christ. Now if anyone builds on this foundation with gold, silver, precious stones, wood, hay, straw, each one's work will become clear; for the Day will declare it, because it will be revealed by fire; and the fire will test each one's work, of what sort it is. If anyone's work which he has built on it endures, he will receive a reward. If anyone's work is burned, he will suffer loss; but he himself will be saved, yet so as through fire (1 Corinthians 3:11-15).

While the unsaved world is experiencing the horrendous seven-year Tribulation period on earth, believers will be standing before their Lord in judgment to receive rewards based on their good works. It should be noted that only believers will experience this judgment, and at no time will their eternal salvation be in jeopardy. Our eternal destiny is secure. In contrast, all unbelievers will stand before the Great White Throne Judgment at the end of the Millennium, during which their eternal destiny will be determined by their works. Because their works cannot save them, all of them will be cast into the lake of fire.

Significance of Good Works

What exactly is a good work? A good work is anything a Christian does for Jesus Christ, such as witnessing, worshiping, being generous, and the like. Jesus made it clear that nothing is too small to be considered a good work. Matthew 10:42 reveals that even giving a cup of cold water to a child would result in divine compensation.

Good works performed with impure motives, however, will not be rewarded.

When it comes to good works, as 1 Corinthians 3:11-15 indicates, the foundation of Jesus Christ must first be in place. This means that no one can accumulate good works until he has accepted salvation through Christ. Once that occurs, a person can build on that foundation with works represented by "gold, silver, precious stones, wood, hay, straw." These works will be tested by fire. The metals and precious stones represent good works performed with right motives. They will survive the test of fire and be rewarded. The wood, hay, and straw represent bad works and will not survive the test. These include good works performed with bad motives, a hidden agenda, or unconfessed sin in one's life.

A number of stories in the Bible illustrate the varying level of rewards that will be handed out. The parable of Luke 19:11-27 explains that Jesus expects a certain quantity of works relative to what has been entrusted to us. It tells of a nobleman who gave an equal amount of money to his servants to invest while he was away. When he returned, he found that one servant had increased the nobleman's original investment by ten times. The nobleman was very pleased and made the servant ruler over ten cities. Another servant increased the nobleman's money by five times and was given charge over five cities. This illustration demonstrates that our rewards will be proportionate to the degree we have used our God-given opportunities to serve Him. All Christians should understand that God expects results from our lives.

Another parable, found in Matthew 25:14-30, tells of a master who gave five talents to one servant and two to another. The servant with five talents earned five more, while the one with two earned two more. In this case, both servants received the same reward because they both made good use of what had been given to them. Likewise, God will hold us accountable for using what talents, abilities, and opportunities He has given us for His service. Fortunately, we have a just God who will treat each believer according to his or her natural abilities. More will be expected from those of higher privilege. "To whom much is given, from him much will be required" (Luke 12:48).

Now, this doesn't mean that the thought of heavenly rewards should be our motivation for serving Christ. Rather, we should be motivated by our love. But at the same time, we should recognize and act on Jesus' challenge to invest wisely in eternity.

> Do not lay up for yourselves treasures on earth, where moth and rust destroy and where thieves break in and steal; but lay up for yourselves treasures in heaven, where neither moth nor rust destroys and where thieves do not break in and steal. For where your treasure is, there your heart will be also (Matthew 6:19-21).

The symbolism in Christ's parables is interesting. Jesus compares Himself to a landowner or even a king who went on a long journey and, after a great while (almost 2000 years so far), returned—at which time he demanded his servants give an accounting and then gave rewards according to their faithfulness, talent, and time spent in labor.

A formula for such a reward might look like this: Our *talent* multiplied by our productive sharing of the *gospel*, multiplied by the amount of *time* we had after our salvation to labor, will equal our *reward*. God keeps a record of our works. He knows what ability we have to serve Him, and He will hold us accountable for how we use our talents and time in His service. Fortunately, He is a just God and will treat each believer "according to what he has done" (2 Corinthians 5:10), based on his or her natural ability.

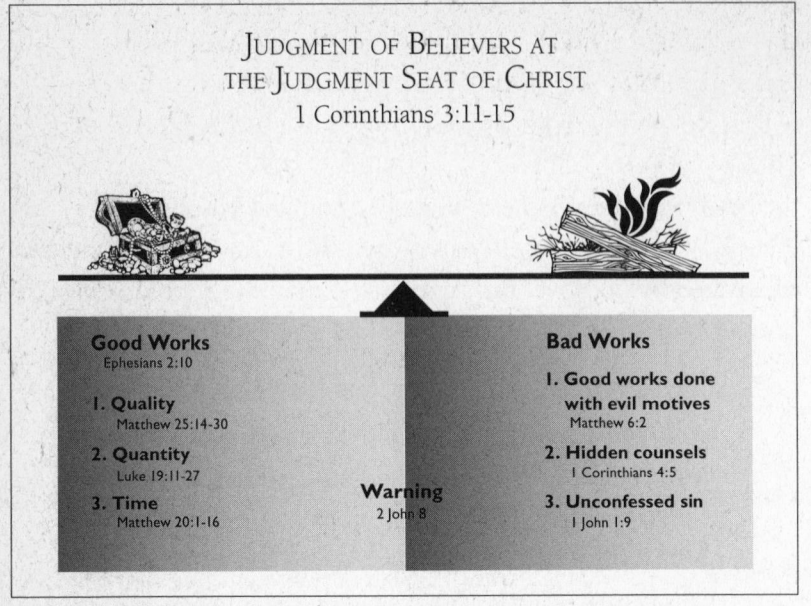

JUDGMENT OF BELIEVERS AT THE JUDGMENT SEAT OF CHRIST
1 Corinthians 3:11-15

Good Works
Ephesians 2:10

1. **Quality**
Matthew 25:14-30

2. **Quantity**
Luke 19:11-27

3. **Time**
Matthew 20:1-16

Warning
2 John 8

Bad Works

1. **Good works done with evil motives**
Matthew 6:2

2. **Hidden counsels**
1 Corinthians 4:5

3. **Unconfessed sin**
1 John 1:9

Excerpted from Tim LaHaye, *Understanding Bible Prophecy for Yourself* (Eugene, OR: Harvest House Publishers, 2001), p. 156.

The Believer's Crowns

Scripture promises crowns to those whose works survive the test of fire at the judgment seat of Christ. Crowns are for rulers, and according to Revelation 20:6, we will rule and reign with Christ in His millennial kingdom. In certain parables, Jesus told of faithful servants who were subsequently appointed to rule over cities. That may be the reason the judgment seat of Christ takes place just prior to His millennial kingdom. Apparently Christians will be assigned to specific areas of service in the kingdom that are proportionate to the good works they performed while alive on earth.

According to the Scriptures, there are at least five types of crowns.

1. The crown of righteousness is for those who live a righteous life—a difficult task in this unrighteous age.

2. The crown of victory is for those who deny themselves the good things in life in order to better serve their Lord.

3. The crown of life is for those who are persecuted and martyred while serving the Lord.

4. The crown of rejoicing is for those who focus their service on winning souls for Christ.

5. The crown of glory is for those who teach the Word of God faithfully to others.

We have seen that a crown is a symbol of rulership and that these crowns are given on the basis of faithful service. The apostle Paul challenged Timothy, "Be watchful in all things" (2 Timothy 4:5). In other words, we are to take advantage of all opportunities to use our talents to the maximum to advance God's kingdom while we are alive on this earth. Any faithful Christian can earn at least one of these crowns, and many will earn several. Let's examine each of these crowns in fuller detail.

The crown of righteousness. God is not able to use many Christians because they do not live righteous lives. Living a righteous life in an unrighteous age isn't easy—it's a constant fight. But the eternal reward will be well worth the effort. Second Timothy 4:8 suggests that if we live in the attitude that our Lord could come soon, we will be driven to live the kind of life He will approve of: "There is laid up for me the crown of righteousness, which the Lord, the righteous Judge, will give to me on that Day, and not to me only but also to all who have loved His appearing."

The incorruptible crown. This "imperishable crown" mentioned in 1 Corinthians 9:25-27 is often called the victor's crown. It is given to the faithful servant who denies himself and his personal desires in order to win the race in faithful service. He doesn't just avoid sin; in order to better serve his Lord, he avoids even some good things that other Christians enjoy.

Paul used runners as an illustration. They deny themselves personal ease and relaxation to arduously train their bodies in order to win their race. Some Christians deny themselves financially to serve the Lord. For example, teachers at Christian schools typically live on tight budgets because their salary is much lower than it would be if they taught in the public sector. Many missionaries deny themselves years of family contact to bring the gospel to places far from home, and the list goes on. This crown seems to be a reward for self-denial.

Moses is a good example of a believer who will probably be given such a crown. He could have remained as the number two man in Egypt, but he didn't.

> By faith Moses, when he became of age, refused to be called the son of Pharaoh's daughter, choosing rather to suffer affliction with the people of God than to enjoy the passing pleasures of sin, esteeming the reproach of Christ greater riches than the treasures in Egypt; for he looked to the reward (Hebrews 11:24-26).

The crown of life. James 1:12 and Revelation 2:10 indicate that there is a special crown for Christians who are persecuted for righteousness' sake. It is sometimes called the martyr's crown, for it goes to those who have been cruelly killed because of their testimony and service for the Master.

God in His sovereignty has chosen to allow the persecution or even martyrdom of some Christians during this church age. He expects people to call on Him by faith in the teaching of His Word rather than by miracles and signs (such as were practiced during the first century, before the Bible was completed). The unjust persecution of fellow believers seems unfair to us, but we can be sure of this: All martyrs will be adequately compensated in the life to come.

The crown of rejoicing. First Thessalonians 2:19 indicates that there is a special soul-winner's crown for those individuals who have led people to faith in Christ. Paul was such an individual. The people to whom he spoke were his "crown of rejoicing" because he had led them to Christ and taught them in the faith. Note that this is called the crown of rejoicing, keeping in mind that the angels in heaven rejoice when a sinner comes to faith (Luke 15:7). In the light of eternity, soul winning is the most important thing in the world. All our busy activity and the things of this earth pale into insignificance in the light of eternity, for in that day the things of the world will be burned up and forgotten, and only what's done for Christ will last.

Almost every church has faithful individuals whose greatest joy is leading people to Christ. They are a minority. They faithfully come out on "visitation night" to share their faith. They witness to those with whom they work, and they pray for God to use them in sharing the gospel. My (Tim's) mother, who went to be with the Lord several years ago, was like that. In fact, when I visited her one week before she died, she asked me to pray for two things: "That the Lord will call me home soon, and that He will use me to lead one more soul to Him before I go." She had her chance three days before she died. While serving as a crisis pregnancy hotline counselor (which she often did), she spoke with a 17-year-old pregnant girl who called in desperation for help. The girl was phone-patched to my mother's home, where, after an hour's conversation, she prayed to receive Christ. Not a bad legacy for my mother to leave her children and grandchildren!

The crown of glory. First Peter 5:1,4 tells us about the elder's crown, or as Peter called it, the crown of glory. There seems to be a special crown for those spiritual elders who share the Word of God. They could be ministers, Sunday school teachers, child evangelism teachers, or anyone else who teaches the Word of God faithfully to others. Such individuals rarely get adequate rewards in this life, but they certainly will be rewarded in the life to come.

Now that we have examined these five crowns, take a few minutes to consider which of these crowns you may receive. Don't live a self-centered, unsurrendered life that will leave you with no crown at all on judgment day. Remember, we are in a race—a long one. Some Christians make good sprinters and serve the Lord well for only a few years. But a wise servant always keeps his body under discipline, lives a holy life year after year, wins as many people to Christ as possible, endures persecution when necessary, and teaches the Word of God at every opportunity. Such a Christian will not regret this kind of life on judgment day!

The judgment seat of Christ will be an exciting experience for the faithful servant of God, but it may be quite sobering for those who lived their lives on earth loving the things of the world to the exclusion of serving their Lord. As the Bible indicates, what we do here on earth will determine how we will serve the Lord during the millennial kingdom. In the final analysis, it is up to each one of us how we will spend those 1000 years.

Serving in the Kingdom

The millennial kingdom will be a time unlike any other in earth's history. Christ Himself will establish a kingdom of peace and prosperity on a newly refurbished earth (2 Peter 3:13), the curse will be lifted from the land, and man's inhumanity to his fellow man will be a thing of the past. Two kinds of people will live on the earth during this period—one natural and one supernatural. There will be those with natural bodies who survived the seven-year Tribulation (including Jews and those who helped the Jews). And there will be those in resurrected, immortal bodies who have come to the earth from heaven with Christ. Those of us in the resurrected bodies will help Jesus rule and reign over those who still possess natural bodies. And our role in helping Jesus Christ rule over this future kingdom will be determined by our actions of today.

Tragically, two of the greatest enemies of Christian service, selfishness and laziness, have cheated many of God's people out of the rewards they could have received. Second John 8 warns us not to "lose those things we worked for." Although we will not lose our salvation, it's possible to forfeit our rewards by yielding to temptation. The Bible says we reap what we sow (see Galatians 6:7). This life serves as a time of planting; the next life includes the harvest. Just as the farmer must work hard in the spring in order to harvest a crop in the fall, we must dedicate ourselves to serving Christ now in order to receive our rewards in eternity. This truth should motivate believers to embrace a life of Christian service.

> Therefore, my beloved brethren, be steadfast, immovable,
> always abounding in the work of the Lord, knowing that
> your labor is not in vain in the Lord (1 Corinthians 15:58).

The Bible makes it clear that God is keeping the records. All who serve the Lord will be rewarded for that service. In addressing this very issue, Jesus promised to reward every believer "according to his works" at the time of His second coming (Matthew 16:27). We should not serve Christ merely to earn rewards, but He assures us that we will indeed be rewarded for our faithful service to Him.

Lesson 5

The Believer's Rewards

Romans 8:1 promises that there is "no condemnation to those who are in Christ Jesus." We do not need to fear punishment for our sins—Christ has paid the price for them. Because of Christ's work on the cross, those who have accepted His gift of salvation will spend eternity in heaven and not in hell.

1. We will not be judged for our sins (a judgment Christ already took for us), but immediately after the rapture, we will face a judgment in which we will be rewarded according to our works on earth. Are you ready for this?

2. Read 1 Corinthians 3:11-15. Who is the foundation upon which we should build (verse 11)?

3. What building materials are listed in verse 12?

4. What will the fire do, according to verse 13?

5. Who will receive a reward (verse 14)?

6. What warning is given in verse 15?

7. The works that will receive rewards are called "good works." We find many examples of good works all through the Bible, but some specific passages are well worth paying attention to. What good works do you find mentioned in Romans 12:9-18?

8. What are we to do—and not do—according to Ephesians 4:29-32?

9. What encouragement are we given about "doing good" in Galatians 6:9?

10. What exhortation are we given in Galatians 6:10?

———✦———

Applying Prophecy to Everyday Life

How should the knowledge that you will one day be rewarded for your works on earth affect the way you live?

6

THE RISE OF THE ANTICHRIST

The Bible clearly predicts the rise of the Antichrist in the end times. As civilization speeds toward its final destiny, the appearance of a powerful world ruler is inevitable. The key question facing our generation is whether he is already alive and moving into power. How can we know who he is? What clues are there to his identity? When will he make his move to control the global economy and world politics?

The Antichrist is a major end-times figure, but the term "Antichrist" appears only in 1 John 2:18-22; 4:3 and 2 John 7. The apostle John uses it both in the singular ("the Antichrist") and in the plural ("many antichrists"). John indicates that his readers have already heard that the Antichrist is coming in the future. Then he surprises them by announcing that many antichrists have already come. He defines these lesser antichrists as liars who deny that Jesus is the Christ (1 John 2:22). In this sense, an antichrist is any false teacher who denies the person and word of Jesus Christ. Such teachers are truly anti (against) Christ.

In 1 John 4:1-3, John warns us to test the spirits to make sure they are from God. Again, he warns that many false prophets have "gone out into the world." These are the people who don't acknowledge that Jesus is from God. In this sense, "the spirit of the Antichrist... is now already in the world."

The Spirit of the Antichrist

We can be certain that in the broadest sense, "the spirit of the Antichrist" is already at work. It does everything it can to undermine, deny, and reject the truth about Jesus Christ. That spirit has been here since the first century, actively opposing the work of Christ on earth.

From the very beginning of the Christian era, believers were convinced that a world ruler would eventually come on the scene who was the embodiment of Satan. Revelation 12–13 presents an unholy trinity that aligns Satan, the Antichrist, and the False Prophet against the Father, the Son, and the Holy Spirit. Thus, the real power behind the Antichrist is Satan. The "father of lies" is the perpetrator of the human manifestation of the world's greatest liar and the source of the lie that will condemn multitudes to divine judgment (2 Thessalonians 2:11).

"Antichrist" in the NIV	
indicates that the end is near	"You have heard that the antichrist is coming, even now many antichrists have come. This is how we know it is the last hour" (1 John 2:18).
denies the Father and the Son	"Such a person is the antichrist—denying the Father and the Son" (1 John 2:22).
does not acknowledge Jesus	"Every spirit that does not acknowledge Jesus is not from God. This is the spirit of the antichrist" (1 John 4:3).
does not acknowledge Jesus came to earth in human form	"Many deceivers, who do not acknowledge Jesus Christ as coming in the flesh, have gone out into the world. Any such person is the deceiver and the antichrist" (2 John 7).

Titles of the Antichrist

The Antichrist is known by several names and titles in the Bible. Each one provides a unique glimpse of his diabolical character and nature. Together, they present a portrait that leaves little to the imagination.

A beast. "I saw a beast rising up out of the sea, having seven heads and ten horns, and on his horns ten crowns, and on his heads a blasphemous name" (Revelation 13:1).

The man of sin. "Let no one deceive you by any means; for that Day will not come unless the falling away comes first, and the man of sin is revealed, the son of perdition" (2 Thessalonians 2:3).

The lawless one. "The lawless one will be revealed, whom the Lord Jesus will consume with the breath of his mouth and destroy with the brightness of his coming" (2 Thessalonians 2:8).

The abomination. "When you see the 'abomination of desolation,' spoken of by Daniel the prophet, standing in the holy place…" (Matthew 24:15).

The little horn. "I was considering the horns, and there was another horn, a little one, coming up among them, before whom three of the first horns were plucked out by the roots. And there, in this horn, were eyes like the eyes of a man, and a mouth speaking pompous words" (Daniel 7:8).

The insolent king. "In the latter time of their kingdom, when the transgressors have reached their fullness, a king shall arise, having fierce features" (Daniel 8:23).

The ruler who is to come. "After the sixty-two weeks Messiah shall be cut off…and the people of the prince who is to come shall destroy the city and the sanctuary" (Daniel 9:26).

The despicable person. "He will be succeeded by a contemptible person who has not been given the honor of royalty. He will invade the kingdom when its people feel secure, and he will seize it through intrigue" (Daniel 11:21 NIV).

The strong-willed king. "The king shall do according to his own will: he shall exalt and magnify himself above every god, shall speak blasphemies against the God of gods, and shall prosper till the wrath has been accomplished; for what has been determined shall be done" (Daniel 11:36).

The worthless shepherd. "I will raise up a shepherd in the land who will not care for those who are cut off, nor seek the young, nor heal those that are broken, nor feed those that still stand. But he will eat the flesh of the fat and tear their hooves in pieces. Woe to the worthless shepherd, who leaves the flock!" (Zechariah 11:16-17).

The Antichrist. "Little children, it is the last hour; and as you have heard that the Antichrist is coming, even now many antichrists have come…Who is a liar, but he who denies that Jesus is the Christ? He is antichrist who denies the Father and the Son" (1 John 2:18,22).

The Nationality of the Antichrist

A great deal has been written about the prefix "anti" in connection with the Antichrist. It can mean either "against" (in opposition to) or "instead of" (in place of). The issue comes down to whether he is the great enemy of Christ or he is a false Christ. If he is the enemy of Christ and the head of a Gentile world government, then he is most likely to be a Gentile himself. If he is a false messiah who is accepted by the Jews, then it would stand to reason that he would be Jewish.

The New Testament does not clearly tell us whether the Antichrist is a Jew or a Gentile. Most prophetic scholars believe he will be a Gentile because…

- He will lead the European Union of Gentile nations (Daniel 7:8-24).
- He will be the leader of the people who destroyed the Temple (the Romans).

- His covenant with Israel will promise Gentile protection for Israel (Daniel 9:27).

- He will rule during the "times of the Gentiles" and their domination over Israel (Luke 21:24).

Both Daniel and Revelation associate the Antichrist with a confederation of ten European nations that correspond in some way to the old Roman Empire. Daniel 2:31-45 symbolizes this by the ten toes of the great statue in Nebuchadnezzar's dream. Daniel 7:19-28 and Revelation 13:1-9 symbolize this by the ten horns on the beast.

In Daniel's prophecies, the Antichrist is always associated with the final phase of the Roman Empire (fourth kingdom). In Revelation 17:9, he is identified with a city that sits on seven hills (Rome). John uses the symbolic term "Babylon the Great" to describe this city, but the mention of seven hills clearly indicates that he is talking about Rome.

It is not difficult, given our current international interconnectedness and the need for a human leader who can guarantee peace among the nations, to imagine a powerful world ruler coming on the scene in the immediate future. The same spirit of Antichrist is at work today, attempting to lure this world into the lap of Satan.

Genius and Power of the Antichrist

The Antichrist will be one of the most astounding leaders the world has ever known. He will demonstrate various kinds of human genius and power:

> intellect (Daniel 7:20)
>
> oratory (Daniel 7:20)
>
> politics (Daniel 11:21)
>
> commerce (Daniel 8:25)
>
> war (Daniel 8:24)

administration (Revelation 13:1-2)

religion (2 Thessalonians 2:4)

Perhaps the most telling of his characteristics is depicted in Daniel 11:21, which tells us that he will come to power and "seize the kingdom by intrigue" ("flatteries" in the KJV). He will be a master of deception, empowered by the father of lies. Many believe he will be Satan incarnate—thus his seemingly miraculous recovery in Revelation 13:3.

Notice the contrasts between Christ and the Antichrist.

Christ	Antichrist
the truth	the lie
holy one	lawless one
man of sorrows	man of sin
Son of God	son of Satan
mystery of godliness	mystery of iniquity
good shepherd	worthless shepherd
exalted on high	cast down to hell
humbled Himself	exalted himself
despised	admired
cleanses the Temple	defiles the Temple
slain for the people	slays the people
the Lamb	the Beast

A simple survey of the characteristics of the Antichrist confirms that he is both a false Christ (*pseudochristos*) and against Christ (*antichristos*). He masquerades as an angel of light only to plunge the world into spiritual darkness. Like Satan, he is a destroyer, not a builder. Promising peace, he pushes the world into war. In every conceivable way, he is just like Satan, who indwells and empowers him.

Is the Antichrist Alive Today?

The spirit of Antichrist is alive and well! It is the Satan-inspired expression of lawlessness and rebellion against God, the things of God, and the people of God. It has been alive since Satan slithered his way around the Garden of Eden. It has been the driving force behind the whole terrible history of the human race—wars, murders, thefts, and exploitation. It is the ugly expression of the destructive nature of the great deceiver himself.

The New Testament authors assure us that the spirit of the Antichrist was active in their day 20 centuries ago. It has remained active throughout the whole of church history, expressing itself in persecutions, heresies, spiritual deceptions, false prophets, and false religions. Satan has battled the church at every turn throughout its long history, waiting for the right moment to indwell the right person—the Antichrist—as his final masterpiece.

Guessing whether a certain contemporary figure might be the Antichrist, however, has always proven futile. Viewing the future through the eyes of the present has led to some bizarre speculations about the identity of the Antichrist: Nero, Charlemagne, Napoleon, Mussolini, Hitler, Stalin, Gorbachev, and even Bill Clinton!

It is too soon to guess the identity of the Antichrist, but one thing is certain—the cry for religious ecumenism (unity) is growing louder all the time. Some have gone so far as to try to label Hindus, Buddhists, and Muslims as fellow believers. But there is a vast difference between the uniqueness of Jesus Christ and the so-called spirituality of other religions. All other religions teach that humans must somehow work their way to God. Christianity teaches that God has worked His way to us by sending His Son to die for our sins. All other religions teach, "Try harder." Christianity teaches, "Give up! Trust God to take care of your spiritual destiny."

Jesus said, "I am the way, the truth, and the life. No one comes to the Father except through Me" (John 14:6). This was His most narrow and dogmatic statement. He was proclaiming His uniqueness in the divine plan of salvation. This claim and our Lord's great commission to evangelize the entire world stand in opposition to all other religious claims. They set Christianity apart from the other world religions because Christianity is based on faith in what Christ did, not faith in what we can do.

We must come to the end of ourselves in order to cast ourselves totally upon God's grace for our salvation. God has made provision for our sins in the sacrifice of His own Son. Jesus' death on the cross was one of substitution. He took our place and died vicariously for our sins. He also rose from the dead to triumph over sin and death, and He offers everlasting life to all who receive Him by faith.

Ecumenical attempts to ally Christianity with non-Christian religions nullify the unique evangelistic appeal of the church. Once we drop our essential beliefs, we have nothing to offer to an unbelieving world. The uniqueness of Christianity is Christ! He is the only incarnate Son of God, who died for the sins of the world and rose again from the dead. Therefore, we ought to proclaim His uniqueness as the only Savior of sinners!

The only real hope to turn our generation away from the mindless pursuit of materialism is to call it back to the spiritual values that give real meaning and purpose to life. That is what Jesus meant when He said, "Seek first the kingdom of God and His righteousness, and all these things shall be added to you" (Matthew 6:33).

Jesus Himself said, "Of that day and hour no one knows, not even the angels of heaven, but My Father only" (Matthew 24:36). The obvious point of this passage is that no one knows the time, so there's no sense in trying to guess when Christ will return. It's far better to be ready all the time because Jesus could come at any time!

Any apparent delay in Christ's return is not due to God's indecision, but to the fact that He has not let us in on the secret. Nor has He revealed this to Satan, who is a limited, finite being. Satan himself is left guessing when the rapture might occur. This means he must have a man in mind to indwell as the Antichrist in every generation. In other words, any one of a number of people could have been the Antichrist, but only one will be. Satan too must keep selecting candidates and waiting for God's timing.

The apostle Paul comments on this in 2 Thessalonians 2:1-12, where he tells us that the "coming of our Lord Jesus" (verse 1) will not happen until the "falling away comes first, and the man of sin is revealed" (verse 3). He then writes, "You know what is holding him back, so that he may be revealed at the proper time" (verse 6 NIV). Only after the rapture of the church will the identity of the Antichrist be revealed. In other words, you don't want to know who he is. If you ever do figure out who he is and you're still here on earth, you've been left behind!

Since Satan must prepare a man to be his crowning achievement in every generation, we should not be surprised that several likely candidates have appeared on the horizon of human history only to vanish away. Satan must wait on God's timing. He can't make his move until God removes the restraining power of the Holy Spirit indwelling the church. The Spirit is the agent and the church is the means by which God restrains Satan's diabolical plan—until the Father calls us home to heaven by means of the rapture.

In the meantime, Satan waits for his opportunity to destroy the whole world and the ultimate plan of God. He may be a defeated foe, but he has every intention of keeping up the fight to the very end. Even now he is moving about restlessly, searching for the right man to be the Antichrist.

Ten Keys to the Antichrist's Identity

The Bible gives us at least ten keys to identifying the Antichrist when he does come to power. They provide enough details to give a general idea of who he will be when Satan inspires him to make his move onto the world scene. These clues also make it clear that only one person in history will fit this description. There have been many prototypes, but there will be only one Antichrist.

1. He will rise to power in the last days: "Later in the time of wrath [the time of the end]...a fierce-looking king, a master of intrigue, will arise" (Daniel 8:19,23 NIV).

2. He will rule the whole world: "Authority was given him over every tribe, tongue, and nation" (Revelation 13:7).

3. His headquarters will be in Rome: "The beast that you saw was, and is not, and will ascend out of the bottomless pit...The seven heads are seven mountains on which the woman sits" (Revelation 17:8-9).

4. He will be intelligent and persuasive: "The other horn... looked more imposing than the others and...had eyes and a mouth that spoke boastfully" (Daniel 7:20 NIV).

5. He will rule by international consent: "The ten horns which you saw are ten kings...These are of one mind, and they will give their power and authority to the beast" (Revelation 17:12-13).

6. He will rule by deception: "He will become very strong... and will succeed in whatever he does...He will cause deceit to prosper, and he will consider himself superior" (Daniel 8:24-25 NIV).

7. He will control the global economy: "No one may buy or sell except one who has the mark or the name of the beast, or the number of his name" (Revelation 13:17).

8. He will make a peace treaty with Israel: "Then he shall

confirm a covenant with many for one week; but in the middle of the week he shall bring an end to sacrifice and offering" (Daniel 9:27).

9. He will break the treaty and invade Israel: "The people of the prince who is to come shall destroy the city and the sanctuary. The end of it shall be with a flood, and till the end of the war desolations are determined" (Daniel 9:26).

10. He will claim to be God: "He will oppose and will exalt himself over everything that is called God or is worshiped, so that he sets himself up in God's temple, proclaiming himself to be God" (2 Thessalonians 2:4 NIV).

The Bible gives many other details regarding the Antichrist. He will administrate the world government and the global economy, assisted by the leader of the world religion (Revelation 13:11-18). He may be moving into power at this very moment. Only time will reveal his true identity.

When the Antichrist does come to power, he apparently will promise world peace through a series of international alliances, treaties, and agreements (see Daniel 8:24; Revelation 17:12). Despite his promises of peace, his international policies will inevitably plunge the world into the greatest war of all time. And at the end of the Tribulation, Christ will return and destroy the Antichrist. The good news for God's people is that he will not come to power until after the rapture.

Lesson 6

The Rise of the Antichrist

Christians are often surprised to discover that more than 100 passages of Scripture describe the Antichrist, who will rise up in the last days. The term "Antichrist" itself is used very little in the Bible, but the Antichrist and the global system he runs are mentioned numerous times.

Through the ages, many people have tried to identify this coming world ruler, but the Bible simply does not give us enough information to make this determination. Instead, we are given some general clues and facts—and it's important that we use discernment and keep these facts separated from the rampant speculation that often occurs in an attempt to figure out who the Antichrist is.

1. Pages 75-76 list 11 different words or phrases the Bible uses to speak of the Antichrist. With reference to these descriptors, what are some general conclusions you can make about the character of this person?

2. According to the explanation on page 76 what is significant about the prefix "anti" in the name Antichrist?

3. Read 2 Thessalonians 2:4. What will the Antichrist oppose? Where will he do this? What will he proclaim about himself?

4. What does God say in Isaiah 45:5-6 about anyone who might try to oppose Him?

5. In Revelation 19:19, we're told the Antichrist ("the beast") will attempt to make war against the Lord. According to verse 20, what will happen to the Antichrist?

6. Read Revelation 13:7. What will be the extent of the Antichrist's authority during his reign?

7. What do we read about the extent of God's authority in each of the following verses?

1 Chronicles 29:11-12

Psalm 10:16

Revelation 19:16

———∞∞∞———

Applying Prophecy to Everyday Life

The Antichrist will wield enormous power and unleash unimaginable cruelty on the world, but we do not need to be fearful of him. The outcome is already certain—Jesus will defeat the Antichrist when He returns, and we will reign with Jesus in His kingdom on earth. How does this knowledge comfort or encourage you?

7

BEWARE OF FALSE PROPHETS

The Antichrist will not rise to power alone. His success will result from a worldwide spiritual deception perpetrated by an associate, the False Prophet, who is also known as the second beast (Revelation 13:11-17). This so-called prophet's ability to perform miraculous signs will enable him to convince people that the Antichrist is the leader for whom they have been looking. The False Prophet will also encourage worldwide worship of the Antichrist (Revelation 19:20; 20:10). In Scripture the False Prophet's identity is not revealed, but Revelation 13 presents ten identifying features that help us to know who he is. The False Prophet...

> rises out of the earth (verse 11)
>
> is motivated by Satan (verse 11)
>
> controls religious affairs (verse 12)
>
> promotes the worship of the beast (verse 12)
>
> performs signs and miracles (verse 13)
>
> deceives the whole world (verse 14)

empowers the image of the beast (verse 15)

kills all who refuse to worship the beast (verse 15)

controls all economic commerce (verse 17)

controls the mark of the beast (verses 17-18)

Bible scholars are divided on whether the False Prophet will be Jewish or Gentile. The biblical record itself is inconclusive on this matter. However, when we observe the relationship of the False Prophet to the great prostitute (Revelation 17), we immediately notice his connection to the city on "seven mountains" (see 17:7,9), "which reigns over the kings of the earth" (verse 18). It seems clear that John is referring to Rome when he describes "Babylon the Great" (verse 5).

> Some believe the idea that he is a Jew is supported by the things said about the second beast regarding his actions and character: (a) this beast is the false prophet who promotes the worship of the first beast by performing signs which are similar to Elijah's, a prophet of Israel (13:12-13), and (b) he has two horns, like a lamb, the sacrificial animal of the Jews. But such a conclusion is not necessary.
>
> However, in the light of the great anti-Semitism of the last half of the Tribulation, it seems unlikely that Satan or the first beast would allow a Jew to live much less occupy such an important position of power and authority. More than likely he is simply an important religious figure representing a rising religious and ecclesiastical movement which this second beast and Satan will use to promote the beast out of the sea (cf. 17:7,15-16). The harlot in chapter 17 refers to religious Babylon, ecclesiastical Rome. The waters there represent the many nations she has influenced...While this apostate religious system will be destroyed by the beast (Revelation 17:16), it appears that the false prophet will, because of his close affinity with the first beast, make it through the entire Tribulation period since Revelation 19:20 shows that

both the first beast and the false prophet are cast alive into the lake of fire together.[1]

Little has been written about the False Prophet compared to the volumes of material about the Antichrist. The Antichrist and the False Prophet are two separate individuals who will work toward a common deceptive goal. Their roles and relationship will be similar to that which was common in the ancient world between a ruler and the high priest of a national religion.

Work of the False Prophet

The False Prophet is depicted in Revelation as one who uses miraculous signs and wonders to deceive the world into worshiping the Antichrist. The False Prophet will extend his ecclesiastical administration over the whole earth by establishing the church of the Antichrist, a counterfeit of the true church.

This apostate religion will be bound together by a shared hatred of genuine Christianity. Thus, the False Prophet does not so much deny Christian doctrine as he corrupts it. Only in this way can the Antichrist sit in the temple of God, demanding to be worshiped as God (2 Thessalonians 2:4; see also Isaiah 14:12-14). Remember, when Satan tempted Christ, he appealed for worship (Matthew 4:8-10). In fact, Satan offered to surrender the entire world to Christ if He would worship him. Therefore, it should not surprise us that the goal of the satanically inspired False Prophet will be to get the whole world to bow down to the Antichrist, who is the personification of Satan himself.

Together, Satan (the dragon), the Antichrist (the beast of the sea), and the False Prophet (the beast of the earth) will comprise an unholy trinity that is a counterfeit of the triune God. Generally speaking, Satan opposes the Father, the Antichrist opposes the Son, and the False Prophet opposes the Holy Spirit. This ungodly alliance will be Satan's final attempt to overthrow the work of God on earth.

The method of this diabolical attempt is explained in the biblical record. The Antichrist dare not appear until after removal of the Restrainer and the resulting "rebellion" (NIV) or "falling away" (KJV) of apostasy (2 Thessalonians 2:3). In the meantime, the spirit of Antichrist (lawlessness) is already at work attempting to pervert the gospel and corrupt the true church. When this process is sufficiently established, the False Prophet will arise to prepare for the coming of the Antichrist.

The False Prophet had "two horns like a lamb and spoke like a dragon" (Revelation 13:11). He looks religious, but he talks like the devil. He counterfeits true religion in order to hide his real identity. Whereas the Holy Spirit is dedicated to bringing the world to know Jesus Christ, the False Prophet is dedicated to bringing all men into spiritual allegiance with the Antichrist.

It should not surprise us then that the False Prophet represents the apostate religion of the end times. If his rise to power parallels that of the Antichrist, he will preside over apostate Christendom after the rapture of true believers to heaven. All who are left behind—regardless of their religious affiliation—will be spiritually blind unbelievers. In such an environment, the False Prophet will have no problem deceiving the whole world. The Holy Spirit will still be omnipresent in the world, but the removal of the church (the body of Christ) will bring His restraining ministry to an end.

The Second Beast

After the revelation of the first beast (the Antichrist), John sees this second beast (the False Prophet) coming up out of the earth and occupying a secondary role that will support the activities of the first beast.

> Then I saw another beast coming up out of the earth, and
> he had two horns like a lamb and spoke like a dragon.

> And he exercises all the authority of the first beast in his presence, and causes the earth and those who dwell in it to worship the first beast, whose deadly wound was healed (Revelation 13:11-12).

In contrast to the first beast, which arises out of the sea, the second beast comes out of the earth. He is of similar nature to the first beast. The same word for "beast" (Greek, *therion*) is used as well as the word "another" (*allo*), meaning "one like in kind." Some have interpreted the word "earth" as referring to the Holy Land, but it is simply the general word for the earth. If the sea, mentioned as the source of the first beast, represents the mass of humanity and indicates the racial background of the first beast as a Gentile, the reference to the second beast as coming out of the earth indicates that the False Prophet (Revelation 19:20) is a creature of earth rather than heaven.

To argue that the earth means Palestine and that therefore this character is a Jew is reading into the passage more than it says. His geographic origin and racial connection are not mentioned. He is pictured, however, as having two horns like a lamb and as speaking like a dragon. The description of him as a lamb seems to indicate that he has a religious character, a conclusion supported by his being named a prophet. His speaking as a dragon indicates that he is motivated by the power of Satan, who is "the dragon."

As a supporting character to the first beast, he is active on behalf of the first beast and exercises his authority. We've seen that Revelation 13:12 reveals he has "all the authority of the first beast in his presence." Using his satanic power, he causes those who dwell in the earth to worship the first beast, whose seemingly mortal wound was healed (verse 3).

Some evidence points to the conclusion that the second beast is the head of the apostate church during the first half of Daniel's seventieth week. With the rise of the first beast to a place of worldwide dominion, the apostate church is destroyed according to Revelation 17:16, and the worship of the whole world is directed to the beast out of the sea. The second beast, however, survives the destruction of the church that had been under his control, and he assists the beast in making the transition. Facilitating this change into the final form of apostate religion, the beast out of the earth causes men to worship the first beast.

The second beast is identified as the head of the apostate church in many ways in the book of Revelation. He is obviously religiously associated with the first beast because his miracles and activities cause men to worship the image of the first beast (cf. 13:13-17). He also clearly shares prominence and leadership with the first beast throughout the Great Tribulation, for they both are cast alive into the lake of fire at its close (19:20).

The Deceiving Miracles of the False Prophet

The first miracle accomplished by the false prophet is described as a great wonder and one of many "great signs." He calls down great fire from heaven in the sight of other people. The miracle may be in connection with Elijah's similar miracle (2 Kings 1:10-12) or to compete with the destructive fire from the mouths of the two witnesses (Revelation 11:5). The Bible notes that the devil has power to perform miracles to mislead people into worshiping the beast.

This misleading power is specifically mentioned in 13:14. He exhibits his powers in the sight of the first beast (the Antichrist). The False Prophet will use his influence to command people to make an image of the first beast, described three times in Revelation 13 as one who was wounded but continues to live.

> The beast is both the empire and its ruler. As ruler he is the symbol of the empire and the executor of its power. Though the wound by the sword apparently refers to the decline of the historic Roman Empire and its revival is

indicated by the expression "did live," the man who serves at the head of the empire is the symbol of this miraculous restoration. The image made to the beast is not necessarily an image of the beast but, like the image of Nebuchadnezzar in Daniel 3, is the symbol of his power and majesty. Though the Scriptures do not say so, it is apparent that this suggestion is followed through, and the image, whatever its character, becomes the center of the false worship of the world ruler. This image, referred to three times in the chapter, is mentioned six more times in the book of Revelation (14:9,11; 15:2; 16:2; 19:20; 20:4). The image is the center of the false worship and the focal point of the final state of apostasy, the acme of the idolatry which has been the false religion of so many generations.[2]

Implementing the Mark of the Beast

One important function of the false prophet will be implementing the mark of the beast.

> He was granted power to give breath to the image of the beast, that the image of the beast should both speak and cause as many as would not worship the image of the beast to be killed. He causes all, both small and great, rich and poor, free and slave, to receive a mark on their right hand or on their foreheads, and that no one may buy or sell except one who has the mark or the name of the beast, or the number of his name. Here is wisdom. Let him who has understanding calculate the number of the beast, for it is the number of a man: His number is 666 (Revelation 13:15-18).

Notice what this mark will include.

1. *It will take place at the midpoint of the Tribulation.*

Therefore, believers today need not worry about whether a certain technology is the mark of the beast.

2. *It will be a universal mark.* Every person on the planet will be required to obtain this mark on his or her head or right hand.

3. *Obtaining the mark will require worship of the beast's image.* Christians and others who refuse to give allegiance will not be able to receive the mark.

4. *This mark will be required to buy or sell.* In today's growing cashless society, it is easy to see a future world without cash or coins. However, in the end times this system will ultimately be manipulated in a manner that will centralize control and permit financial exchange only to those with the mark.

5. *Those who will not worship the beast's image will be persecuted and killed.* Those who choose to stand against worship of the Antichrist in the last days will face an enormous struggle.

6. *The identity of the mark is 666.* Many have sought to understand the meaning of this number. Much is unknown, but the number of the name of the Antichrist clearly must add up to 666. It is not merely three sixes. No one thus far in history properly qualifies for this identification. The number likely indicates that 666 will refer to the evil world ruler (the Antichrist) in the tribulation period.

The Great Lie

The apostle Paul explained, "For the secret power of lawlessness is already at work; but the one who now holds it back will continue to do so till he is taken out of the way" (2 Thessalonians 2:7 NIV). After the rapture, the Holy Spirit will still convict people of sin, but

His restraining ministry will be over, and all of Satan's evil will break loose on earth. Then the lawless one will be revealed. Paul added more information: "The coming of the lawless one will be in accordance with how Satan works. He will use all sorts of displays of power through signs and wonders that serve the lie, and all the ways that wickedness deceives those who are perishing" (verses 9-10 NIV). The rise of the Antichrist will correspond with a general breakdown in religious and moral values, resulting in a decadent society that will believe the lie rather than the truth. The apostle Paul does not define the lie, but he specifies that it is a particular lie, not just any lie. It is possible that this could refer to a falsehood perpetrated to explain away the rapture (such as a claim that those who disappeared were abducted by aliens). But it is more likely that the lie is the official rejection of Christ and the deification and worship of the Antichrist.

The False Prophet is presented in Revelation as an individual who is empowered by Satan (13:11-12). The religious system that he represents is called the "great harlot" (17:1) who is drunk with the "blood of God's holy people" (17:6 NIV). Therefore, the final phase of apostasy refers to both a religious system and the individual who leads it.

The Master of Deceit

The Bible describes Satan as the "father of lies" (John 8:44 NIV) and the ultimate deceiver. His name means "accuser," and he is depicted as the accuser of God and His people (Revelation 12:10). He is opposed to God and seeks to alienate people from the truth. He misled the fallen angels (Revelation 12:3-4) and tempts men and women to sin against God's laws (Genesis 3:1-13; 1 Timothy 6:9). He denies and rejects the truth of God and deceives those who perish without God (2 Thessalonians 2:10). Ultimately, he inspires the false prophets and the very spirit of the Antichrist (1 John 2:18-23).

The Bible clearly warns us that in the last days people will "abandon the faith and follow deceiving ['seducing,' KJV] spirits and things ['doctrines,' KJV] taught by demons" (1 Timothy 4:1 NIV). These false teachings will come through hypocritical liars whose minds have been captured by Satan's lies (1 Timothy 4:2). So the False Prophet will not be alone in his deception; there will be many other false prophets in the last days.

What are the characteristics of false prophets? How can we recognize them? The Bible describes them in several ways.

Self-deceived. Some false teachers may be sincere, but because their message is wrong, they themselves are wrong. They have deceived themselves into believing their false messages. Their messages come from within their own minds and are not from God.

Liars. Some false prophets are deliberate liars who have no intention of telling the truth. The apostle John says, "Who is a liar but he who denies that Jesus is the Christ? He is antichrist who denies the Father and the Son" (1 John 2:22).

Heretics. These are people who preach heresy (false doctrine) and divide the church. Of them John said, "They went out from us, but they were not of us" (1 John 2:19). The apostle Peter said, "There will be false teachers among you, who will secretly bring in destructive heresies…[These men] speak evil of the things they do not understand" (2 Peter 2:1,12).

Scoffers. There are some who do not necessarily promote false teaching so much as they outright reject the truth of God. Of them the Bible warns, "Scoffers will come in the last days, walking according to their own lusts" (2 Peter 3:3). The apostle Paul calls them "lovers of themselves…boasters, proud…haughty" (2 Timothy 3:2,4). Jude calls them "grumblers, complainers" (verse 16).

Blasphemers. Those who speak evil of God, Christ, the Holy Spirit, the people of God, the kingdom of God, and the attributes of God are called blasphemers. Jude calls them godless men who "slander whatever they do not understand…They are clouds without rain…trees, without fruit…wild waves of the sea…wandering stars" (verses 10,12-13 NIV). The apostle Paul said that he himself was a blasphemer before his conversion to Christ (1 Timothy 1:13).

Seducers. Jesus warned that some false prophets will perform miraculous signs and wonders to seduce or deceive the very elect if possible (Mark 13:22). Our Lord's implication is that spiritual seduction is a very real threat even to believers. This would account for the fact that a few genuine but deceived believers may be found among the cults.

Reprobates. This term means "disapproved," "depraved," or "rejected." In Romans 1 Paul refers to those who have rejected the truth of God and turned to spiritual darkness. Consequently, God has given them over to a "reprobate mind" (verse 28 KJV). They have so deliberately rejected God that they have become "filled with all unrighteousness" (verse 29). As a result, they are "haters of God" (verse 30), whose behavior is "undiscerning, untrustworthy, unloving, unforgiving" (verse 31). These people are so far gone spiritually that they know it and don't care.

In Jesus' prophetic Olivet Discourse (Matthew 24–25), He warned, "Take heed that no one deceives you...many will be offended... many false prophets will rise up and deceive many...false christs and false prophets will rise and show great signs and wonders" (Matthew 24:4,10-11,24). Our Lord warned His disciples and us of the possibility of spiritual seduction by false prophets and teachers, especially as the end of the age approaches.

Spiritual deception is the goal of the False Prophet as he encourages people to embrace the social, economic, and religious program of the Antichrist. These sweeping changes will occur rapidly with the help of television and the Internet. As we approach the end of the age, then, we can fully expect that false prophets and spiritual darkness will engulf the world.

Lesson 7

Beware of False Prophets

The Antichrist, in his bid to rule the world, will have the help of "the second beast," or the False Prophet, who is described in Revelation 13:11-17. This False Prophet's main role will be to give the Antichrist an appearance of credibility, to deceive the world into worshiping the Antichrist.

Little is written in the Bible about the False Prophet himself, but a lot is said about the danger of false prophets in general. The Bible's warnings reveal the enormous seriousness of what the False Prophet will do during the last days.

1. What did Jesus say in Matthew 7:15 about the outward appearance and true inner nature of false prophets?

2. According to the apostle Paul in 2 Timothy 4:3-4, what will people turn away from, and what will they listen to instead?

3. In Ephesians 4:14, how does Paul describe false teachers?

4. Read 2 Peter 2:1-3. What three things will false prophets do? How will they do this?

5. Read 2 Peter 2:12-17. What are some ways Peter describes false prophets? Why do you think Peter uses such strong language?

———— ᘓᘏᘍ ————

Applying Prophecy to Everyday Life

What are some ways we can protect ourselves against false teachers, according to these verses?

2 Peter 3:14

2 Peter 3:18

2 Timothy 3:10,14-17

8

THE TRIBULATION PERIOD

Jesus warned His disciples that in the last days there would be a period of time more horrific and traumatic than any other in human history. He was, of course, referring to the Great Tribulation.

> There will be great tribulation, such as has not been since the beginning of the world until this time, no, nor ever shall be (Matthew 24:21).

The disciples were familiar with this prophesied time of anguish, for many of the Hebrew prophets of old had warned Israel about a future period of intense suffering. The prophet Jeremiah called it "the time of Jacob's trouble" (Jeremiah 30:7). The Bible uses a variety of names for the Tribulation:

> "the day of the Lord" (1 Thessalonians 5:2)
> the seventieth week of Daniel (Daniel 9:27)
> "a day of devastation and desolation" (Zephaniah 1:15)
> "the wrath to come" (1 Thessalonians 1:10)

"the hour of His judgment" (Revelation 14:7)

"great tribulation" (Matthew 24:21)

The Tribulation is mentioned in more than 60 passages in the Bible. More space is allotted to it than any other subject except for salvation and the second coming of Christ.

Both the prophet Daniel and the apostle John stated this period would last seven years (Daniel 9:24-27; Revelation 11:2-3). After rising to power, the evil "prince who is to come" (Daniel 9:26), the Antichrist, will make a covenant with Israel. This event will signal the beginning of the seven-year Tribulation period. Three and a half years into the Tribulation, at the halfway point, the Antichrist will break the covenant by desecrating the rebuilt Temple in Jerusalem. This will usher in the Great Tribulation, a period of suffering and terror worse than any that mankind has ever experienced in history. Although the Tribulation lasts only seven years, the devastations unleashed during that time will seem endless to those who must face them.

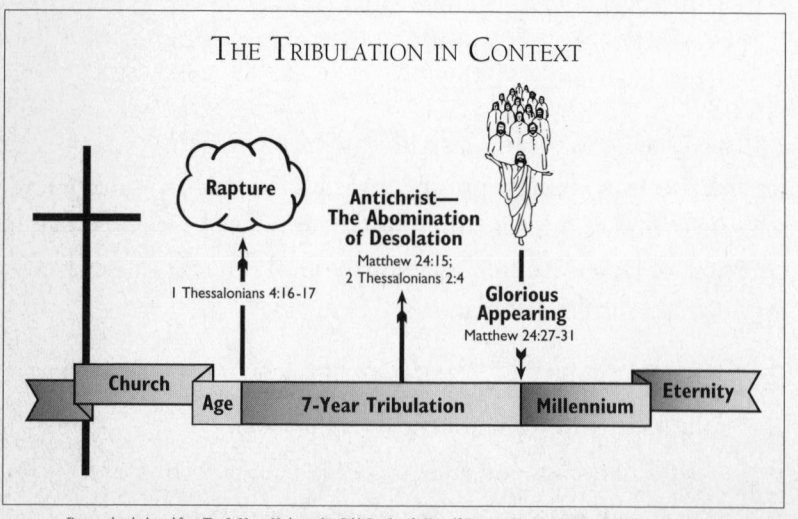

THE TRIBULATION IN CONTEXT

Rapture

Antichrist—
The Abomination
of Desolation
Matthew 24:15;
2 Thessalonians 2:4

I Thessalonians 4:16-17

Glorious
Appearing
Matthew 24:27-31

Church
Age
7-Year Tribulation
Millennium
Eternity

Excerpted and adapted from Tim LaHaye, *Understanding Bible Prophecy for Yourself* (Eugene, OR: Harvest House Publishers, 2001), p. 135.

The Nature of the Tribulation

Through various prophetic passages found in the Bible, we learn that the Tribulation will be a time of...

- *judgment* for those who reject the Savior
- *conclusion* for those who rebel against God
- *decision* for those who will be forced to choose between Christ and the Antichrist
- *chaos* designed to shake mankind's false sense of security
- *revival*, resulting in the greatest soul harvest in history

When will the Tribulation take place? Although no exact date is given, the Bible indicates in Matthew 24:29-31 that it must occur immediately before the glorious appearing of Christ, when Jesus Himself returns to earth to destroy the Antichrist. It will occur after the rapture of the church, when all those who have placed their trust in Jesus Christ will be instantly removed from the planet in order to meet the Lord in the air (1 Thessalonians 4:15-18).

Those who view the Tribulation as primarily a time of wrath overlook the fact that it is also a time of mercy and grace. The Lord is not an angry monster, heaping catastrophes on the heads of innocent men and women. In reality, the people who suffer the judgments of God during the Tribulation are not innocent. These rebels not only reject God and His free offer of salvation but also indulge in every vile sin known to mankind, including the massacre of those who come to Christ during this time. Even then, God's hope is that those who oppose Him will at some point turn to Him. The Tribulation judgments therefore serve a dual purpose: to punish hardened sinners and to move others to repentance. The following Scripture passage exemplifies this truth.

> I will show wonders in the heavens and in the earth: Blood
> and fire and pillars of smoke. The sun shall be turned into

darkness, and the moon into blood, before the coming of the great and awesome day of the LORD. And it shall come to pass that whoever calls on the name of the LORD shall be saved (Joel 2:30-32).

The Tribulation Saints

The untold millions who miss the rapture because of their rejection of God will still have an opportunity to become saved.

After these things I looked, and behold, a great multitude which no one could number, of all nations, tribes, peoples, and tongues, standing before the throne and before the Lamb, clothed with white robes, with palm branches in their hands (Revelation 7:9).

These Tribulation saints, whose numbers are so large they can't be counted, come to the Lord as a result of Tribulation events, demonstrating that our holy God will continue to show His love and mercy to mankind even in the last days. A heavenly being explained that the multitude in white robes represent "the ones who come out of the great tribulation" (Revelation 7:14). No wonder the apostle Peter was able to write, "The Lord is not slack concerning His promise, as some count slackness, but is longsuffering toward us, not willing that any should perish but that all should come to repentance" (2 Peter 3:9).

Those Left Behind

In many respects, the rapture will set the stage for the coming Tribulation. When millions upon millions of Christians disappear from the face of the earth, the world will fall into a state of shock and chaos that defies comprehension. This will prepare the way perfectly for the rise of the Antichrist. He will come to power peaceably using diplomacy, as represented by the rider on the white horse, the first of the four horsemen of the Apocalypse (Revelation 6:1-2). His charm and outward compassion will bring badly needed comfort to a populace on the brink of mass hysteria.

The controlled media will be used to effectively coerce the world into adopting this new leader as the man of the hour. Ongoing efforts to discredit the Bible, which predicted the rapture and the rise of the Antichrist, will be a top priority of the new world government. Every attempt will be made to convince the confused populace that those who have been left behind are the lucky ones even though nothing could be further from the truth.

The spiritual vacuum left by the disappearance of millions of Christians will also enable the Antichrist to further his plan for a forced one-world religion. This pagan religion will unite all religions—with the lone exception of biblical Christianity—into one. In the midst of all this, the Holy Spirit will work through the 144,000 evangelists and the two witnesses in Jerusalem to draw countless numbers of people to Christ during the Tribulation—despite the fact that such a choice will most likely result in martyrdom.

The 144,000 Witnesses

The seventh seal introduces the seven trumpet judgments, which is why many prophecy students consider these judgments to be chronological. The first six seals cover 21 months, and then the breaking of the seventh seal introduces the seven trumpet judgments, which take place during the second quarter (the second 21 months) of the first half of the Tribulation. The sealing of the 144,000 "servants of our God" (Revelation 7:3) probably occurs at the beginning of this period, and they witness all during it, along with the special two witnesses described in Revelation 11.

The Two Witnesses

In the last days, God will have the gospel message proclaimed worldwide so that people are without excuse about making a decision for Christ. During the first half of the Tribulation God uses not only 12,000 Israelites from each of the 12 tribes—a total of 144,000 who reach "a great multitude which no one could number" (Revelation 7:9)—but also two special witnesses near Jerusalem who are endowed with supernatural powers (Revelation 11:3-6).

During the Tribulation, two powerful opposing forces will be at work during the same time: the 144,000 servants of God who will bring forth a mighty soul harvest, and the enormous sinfulness of those who refuse to repent. It will be the same as in our day, with the church witnessing for the Lord on the one hand and those who reject the Savior on the other, except that the opposing forces will be intensified during the Tribulation period.

Also, because the civil government described in Revelation 13 will be under the control of Antichrist and his evil forces, Christians will be persecuted and martyred in large numbers. Many people will become saved through the soul harvest, but for a while, it will seem as if Christians are on the losing end of the battle because the Antichrist is in control of the world. However, we know that ultimately, Christ and His people will be victorious.

World War III

After his peaceful ascension to power, the Antichrist will initiate what we might call World War III (Revelation 6:3-4) against three of the ten regional leaders who will be in power during this time. Death and destruction will be brought to this earth on an unprecedented scale. This battle may involve a nuclear exchange and will be followed by widespread inflation, famine, and disease. Possibly due in part to nuclear fallout, plagues will sweep across the land, and death will come to a fourth of the world's population (Revelation 6:5-8). All the while, the Antichrist will be carrying out his vengeance against those who have chosen to follow Christ instead of him (Revelation 6:9-11). And the genocide of Tribulation saints will escalate as the world sinks further into death and despair.

Up to this point, the judgments that have come upon earth during the Tribulation have been largely the result of man's endeavors. From here onward, however, the judgments will be acts of divine retribution. Revelation 6:12-15 describes an earthquake so massive that "every mountain and island was moved out of its place" (verse 14). The sky will darken and the moon will appear red, apparently because of a series of massive volcanic eruptions. The apostle John also writes of meteor-like objects crashing down onto the earth. So incredible are these events that earth's inhabitants will realize they are witnessing God's judgments right before their eyes.

> The kings of the earth, the great men, the rich men, the commanders, the mighty men, every slave and every free man, hid themselves in the caves and in the rocks of the mountains, and said to the mountains and rocks, "Fall on us and hide us from the face of Him who sits on the throne and from the wrath of the Lamb! For the great day of His wrath has come, and who is able to stand?" (Revelation 6:15-17).

Then hail, fire, and blood will rain down from the sky, causing a third of the earth's trees and grass to burn up. Two more meteors will fall from the sky and kill a third of the sea life, destroy a third of the ships at sea, and poison a third of the earth's fresh water supply. Darkness will continue to envelop the land as the light from the sun and moon is dimmed by a third.

Hell on Earth

Revelation 9 describes a plague of locust-like creatures that descend upon the earth and sting people. For five months, these creatures will torment but not kill unbelievers.

> Out of the smoke locusts came upon the earth. And to them was given power, as the scorpions of the earth have power. They were commanded not to harm the grass of the earth, or any green thing, or any tree, but only those men who do not have the seal of God on their foreheads. And they were not given authority to kill them, but to torment them for five months. Their torment was like the torment of a scorpion when it strikes a man. In those days men will seek death and will not find it; they will desire to die, and death will flee from them (Revelation 9:3-6).

If that weren't enough, armies of demonic horsemen will then be unleashed and kill another third of the world's population (Revelation 9:13-19). And then it gets worse.

The Mark of the Beast

As we have seen, halfway into the Tribulation, the Antichrist will break his treaty with the nation of Israel, desecrate the rebuilt Temple in Jerusalem, and kill the two witnesses who have been proclaiming the gospel (Revelation 11:3-12). He will then seize total control of the monetary system of the world, requiring all to carry his mark, which in some way will consist of the number 666. This is the prophesied mark of the beast, and without it, no one will be able to buy or sell.

> He causes all, both small and great, rich and poor, free and slave, to receive a mark on their right hand or on their foreheads, and that no one may buy or sell except one who has the mark or the name of the beast, or the number of his name.
>
> Here is wisdom. Let him who has understanding calculate the number of the beast, for it is the number of a man: His number is 666 (Revelation 13:16-18).

Even a few short years ago, such a prospect would have seemed inconceivable. But now, with computerized electronic financial transactions occurring worldwide, the ability to control and track the purchases of every human being is not only possible but inevitable.

Preparing for Armageddon

Meanwhile, as the Tribulation progresses, the judgments of God will continue to afflict the ungodly. Loathsome sores will break out on those who have the mark of the beast. The sea and remaining freshwater will be turned into blood. Heat from the sun will scorch the unrepentant, and darkness will envelop the kingdom of the Antichrist (Revelation 16:2-11).

Then the Euphrates River will dry up, allowing the armies of the east to march unhindered to Israel to begin the Battle of Armageddon. The bloodshed will reach unparalleled proportions. A tremendous earthquake will level the cities of the world, and hailstones weighing as much as 100 pounds will fall to the earth. Unfortunately, many of the ungodly still will not repent, despite the severity of these judgments.

> There was a great earthquake, such a mighty and great earthquake as had not occurred since men were on the earth. Now the great city was divided into three parts, and the cities of the nations fell. And great Babylon was remembered before God, to give her the cup of the wine of the fierceness of His wrath. Then every island fled away, and the mountains were not found. And great hail from heaven fell upon men, each hailstone about the weight of a talent. Men blasphemed God because of the plague of the hail, since that plague was exceedingly great (Revelation 16:18-21).

And with that, the judgments will draw to an end. The glorious appearing of Christ comes next. He will be in the air accompanied by the armies of heaven, which consist of all those who were raptured to heaven (Revelation 19:11-14). Christ will then descend to earth in power and glory to win the Battle of Armageddon. He will cast the Beast (the Antichrist) and the False Prophet into the lake of fire and bind Satan in the abyss for 1000 years. Then He will initiate His millennial reign on earth (Revelation 19:19–20:3).

Understanding the Judgments

The book of Revelation includes three sets of seven judgments—21 total judgments that will unfold during the seven-year tribulation period. These have been discussed in this chapter, yet an overview of these judgments provides a helpful understanding of how these events will unfold. The three sets of judgments include the seal judgments, the trumpet judgments, and the bowl (or vial) judgments.

Seal Judgments (Revelation 6, 8)

Seal 1: the rider on the white horse (the Antichrist)

Seal 2: the rider on the red horse (conflict)

Seal 3: the rider on the black horse (inflation and famine)

Seal 4: the rider on the pale horse (death)

Seal 5: the martyred Tribulation saints

Seal 6: a great earthquake

Seal 7: silence in heaven and the beginning of the trumpet judgments

Trumpet Judgments (Revelation 8–9, 11)

Trumpet 1: One-third of the vegetation is destroyed.

Trumpet 2: One-third of the sea is turned into blood.

Trumpet 3: One-third of the waters are contaminated.

Trumpet 4: One-third of the sky is darkened.

Trumpet 5 (the "first woe"): Locust-like creatures plague the earth.

Trumpet 6 (the "second woe"): An army destroys one-third of all people.

Trumpet 7 (the "third woe"): The seven bowl judgments begin.

Bowl Judgments (Revelation 16)

Bowl 1: Terrible sores appear on those who follow the Antichrist.

Bowl 2: All the seas are turned to blood.

Bowl 3: All fresh water is turned to blood.

Bowl 4: The earth is scorched.

Bowl 5: Darkness covers the earth.

Bowl 6: The Euphrates River dries up, and an army marches toward Armageddon.

Bowl 7: A massive earthquake is followed by 100-pound hailstones.

What Begins the Tribulation?

The prophecy of Daniel 9:27 tells us exactly what will start the Tribulation: The prince who is to come "shall confirm a covenant with many for one week." The Antichrist will make a covenant with the nation of Israel to ensure their protection. However, he will break this covenant after three and a half years. This does not mean that the treaty itself will be a seven-year treaty, as opposed to one of indefinite length, but that it will be broken in the middle of the seventieth "week" of Daniel 9:27. Since the seventieth "seven" refers to the seven years of the Tribulation period, the reader understands that the treaty will be broken at the halfway point. But this does not mean that the treaty itself is merely a seven-year treaty.

Daniel's prophecy may relate to the rider on the white horse of

Revelation 6, who comes in peace, for he has no arrows or implements of war in his hand. It appears that the Antichrist will offer peace to the world and make a covenant with Israel, bringing peace to the Jewish people, who will then be able to rebuild their Temple and reinstate their sacrifices—but only for three and a half years! "In the middle of the week [of years] he shall bring an end to sacrifice and offering. And on the wing of abominations shall be one who makes desolate" (Daniel 9:27). The Antichrist will break his covenant with the Jews in the middle of the Tribulation (as we also see in Revelation 11 and 13) and will launch the worst desolation in the history of the world. How long will it last? Daniel 9:27 continues, "Until the consummation, which is determined." This is the same as "the time of the end" (8:17), meaning the end of the 70 weeks or 490 years, when God's dealings with the Jews are consummated and Christ returns to set up His kingdom.

In summary, then, the Tribulation will begin with the signing of the covenant of peace between the coming new world government (headed by the Antichrist) and the nation of Israel. Halfway through the seven years, the Antichrist will break that covenant and persecute the nation of Israel, which will become "desolate."

Many Christians think that the rapture of the church begins the Tribulation. The rapture and the signing of the covenant may take place very close together, but the Bible is not specific on that subject. Still, there has never been a world ruler who has made a covenant of peace with Israel and then broken that covenant after three and a half years. This obviously means that the fulfillment of these events are still future.

Lesson 8

The Tribulation Period

"You ain't seen nothin' yet." This phrase could aptly be used to describe the Tribulation. The horrors of this future time of judgment will be of a magnitude far beyond any cataclysmic event in history. Even the most widespread and devastating of wars to date will pale by comparison to all that will happen during the Tribulation, which will culminate in the war of all wars, Armageddon.

The Bible affirms the tremendous significance of the Tribulation by giving it a lot of attention. More is said about this seven-year period of wrath than about the 1000-year millennial kingdom, heaven, or hell. We find mention of it in the Old Testament at least 49 times and at least 15 times in the New Testament.

1. The Tribulation is referred to by many names in the Bible. What names or descriptive phrases are used in these passages?

   Isaiah 34:8

   Daniel 12:1

   Zephaniah 1:15

   Revelation 3:10

2. What do those verses teach you about the nature of the Tribulation?

3. In the book of Daniel, the term "week" refers to seven years. What will initiate this "week," or the Tribulation, according to Daniel 9:27?

4. What will happen at the middle of the seven-year Tribulation (see Daniel 9:27; Matthew 24:15)?

5. What will occur at the end of the Tribulation (see Revelation 19:11-21)?

6. The Tribulation will be a time of judgment, but it will also be the last clarion call for the lost to receive Jesus Christ as their Savior. Briefly describe the instruments God will use to spread the gospel during this time.

Revelation 7:4-8

Revelation 11:3

Revelation 14:6-7

Applying Prophecy to Everyday Life

The people who are saved during the Tribulation will comprise "a great multitude which no one could number" (Revelation 7:9). Indeed, in the midst of the extreme horrors of the Tribulation, God will call to Himself many, many more people—a testimony of just how loving and merciful He is, giving people ample opportunity to repent of their sins.

Do you have a compassion for the lost? Whom could you be praying for or reaching out to with the message of salvation in Christ?

9

THE GLORIOUS APPEARING

The second coming of Christ is the most anticipated event in human history. The glorious appearing (Titus 2:13) is the ultimate fulfillment of our Lord's promise to return. It is also the culmination of all biblical prophecy. The return of Christ is the final apologetic! Once He returns, there will be no further need to debate His claims or the validity of the Christian message. The King will come in person to set the record straight.

Revelation 19 is probably the most dramatic chapter in all the Bible. It is the capstone to the death and resurrection of Christ. In this chapter we see the living Savior return to earth to crush all satanic opposition to the truth. He will establish His kingdom on earth, fulfilling Old Testament prophecies and His own promise to return.

Just before the crucifixion, the disciples asked Jesus, "What will be the sign of Your coming, and of the end of the age?" (Matthew 24:3). Our Lord replied, "Immediately after the tribulation of those days...the powers of the heavens will be shaken. Then the sign of the Son of Man will appear in heaven, and then all the tribes of the earth will mourn, and they will see the Son of Man coming on the clouds of heaven with power and great glory" (verses 29-30).

As Jesus looked down the corridor of time to the end of the present age, He warned of a time of great tribulation that would come upon the whole world (verses 5-28). He explained that the devastation will be so extensive that unless those days were cut short, "no flesh would be saved" (verse 22). Jesus further said that during this coming day of trouble, the sun and moon will be darkened and "the powers of the heavens will be shaken" (verse 29). His description runs parallel to that found in Revelation 16:1-16, where the final hour of the Tribulation includes atmospheric darkness, air pollution, and ecological disaster.

The return of Christ will mark both the total defeat of the Antichrist and the total triumph of Christ. Without Christ, there is no hope of a better future. He is the central figure of the world to come. It is His kingdom, and we are His bride.

The Promise of Christ's Return

In the upper room, Jesus promised His disciples that He was going to heaven to prepare a place for them. Then He said, "If I go and prepare a place for you, I will come again, and receive you unto myself; that where I am, there ye may be also" (John 14:3 KJV). Even though the early disciples eventually died, the Bible promises, "Behold, I show you a mystery; we shall not all sleep [die], but we shall all be changed [resurrected or raptured], in a moment, in the twinkling of an eye, at the last trump: for the trumpet shall sound, and the dead shall be raised incorruptible, and we shall be changed" (1 Corinthians 15:51-52 KJV).

The apostle Paul reiterates this same hope as he comments about those believers who have already died and gone to heaven.

> If we believe that Jesus died and rose again, even so them also which sleep [die] in Jesus will God bring with him

[from heaven]…For the Lord himself shall descend from
heaven with a shout, with the voice of the archangel, and
with the trump of God: and the dead in Christ shall rise
first: then we which are alive and remain shall be caught
up together with them in the clouds, to meet the Lord in
the air (1 Thessalonians 4:14-17 KJV).

The promise to return for the church (believers of the church age)
is a reference to the rapture. Jesus specifically promises to return personally and physically to take His church up to heaven! When Revelation 19 opens, the church is already in heaven with Christ at the
marriage supper. The rapture has already occurred. Jesus is depicted
as the groom and the church as the bride. The marriage supper cele-
brates their union after the rapture and before their return to earth.

One of the greatest interpretive problems for nonrapturists is
to explain how the church got to heaven prior to the second coming. Surely they are not all martyred, or Paul's comment about "we
who are alive and remain" (1 Thessalonians 4:15) would be mean-
ingless. The rapture must be presumed to have occurred before the
events in Revelation 19, amillennialists and postmillennialists not-
withstanding.

The position of the church (bride of the Lamb) in Revelation
19:7-10 in heaven is crucial to the interpretation of the entire Apocalypse. The church is not mentioned during the seal, trumpet, and
bowl judgments because the church is not on earth when they are
poured out. The term "church" (Greek, *ekklesia*) appears 19 times in
Revelation 1–3. But it does not appear again until Revelation 22:16.
In the meantime, the church appears in Revelation 19:7-10 as the
bride of the Lamb.

The concept of the church as the bride or wife of Christ is clearly
stated in Ephesians 5:25-26, where husbands are admonished to
love their wives as Christ loved the church and gave Himself for her
that He might present her in heaven as a glorious bride. There can

be no doubt, therefore, that John intends us to see the Lamb's "wife" as the church—the bride of Christ.

The Nature of Christ's Return

Jesus promised to return not only for His church but also to judge the world and to establish His kingdom on earth. His half-brother James refers to believers as "heirs of the kingdom which He promised to those who love Him" (James 2:5). Jesus Himself told His disciples that He would not drink the fruit of the vine after the last supper until He drank it with them in His Father's kingdom (Matthew 26:29). After the resurrection, the disciples asked Jesus, "Will You at this time restore the kingdom to Israel?" (Acts 1:6). Jesus replied that the time was in the Father's hands. All these references imply a future kingdom when Christ returns.

Here are ten details of Christ's return.

1. *He will return personally.* The Bible says that "the Lord Himself will descend from heaven" (1 Thessalonians 4:16). Jesus promised He will return in person (Matthew 24:30).

2. *He will appear as the Son of Man.* Since Pentecost, Christ has ministered through the Holy Spirit (John 14:16-23; 16:7-20). But when He returns, He will appear as the Son of Man in His glorified human form (Matthew 24:30; 26:64; see also Daniel 7:13-14).

3. *He will return literally and visibly.* In Acts 1:11 the angels promised, "This same Jesus, who was taken up from you into heaven, will so come in like manner." Revelation 1:7 tells us, "Every eye will see Him, even they who pierced Him. And all the tribes of the earth will mourn." Nowhere in Scripture is there a suggestion that Christ's second coming in power and great glory will be anything but visible and physical. In fact, all unbelievers on the earth at the

time of Christ's return will be eyewitnesses to it. Preterists, who claim Christ has already returned, cannot point to a time when anyone has ever witnessed such.

4. *He will come suddenly and dramatically.* Paul warned, "The day of the Lord so comes as a thief in the night" (1 Thessalonians 5:2). Jesus said, "As the lightning comes from the east and flashes to the west, so also will the coming of the Son of Man be" (Matthew 24:27).

5. *He will come on the clouds of heaven.* Jesus said, "They will see the Son of Man coming on the clouds of heaven" (Matthew 24:30). Luke 21:27 and Daniel 7:13 make the same prediction. Revelation 1:7 says, "Behold, He is coming with clouds."

6. *He will come in a display of glory.* Matthew 16:27 promises, "The Son of Man will come in the glory of His Father." Matthew 24:30 adds, "They will see the Son of Man coming...with power and great glory."

7. *He will come with all His angels.* Jesus promised He would "send His angels with a great sound of a trumpet" (Matthew 24:31). He said in one of His parables, "The reapers are the angels...so it will be at the end of this age" (Matthew 13:39-40).

8. *He will come with His bride, the church.* That, of course, is the whole point of Revelation 19. Colossians 3:4 adds, "When Christ who is our life appears, then you also will appear with Him in glory." Zechariah 14:5 says, "The Lord my God will come, and all the saints with You."

9. *He will return to the Mount of Olives.* "In that day His feet will stand on the Mount of Olives" (Zechariah 14:4). Where the glory of God ascended into heaven, it will return (Ezekiel 11:23). Where Jesus ascended into heaven, He will return (Acts 1:9-11).

10. *He will return in triumph and victory.* Zechariah 14:9

states, "The LORD shall be King over all the earth." Revelation 19:16 depicts him as "King of kings and Lord of lords." He will triumph over the Antichrist, the False Prophet, and Satan (Revelation 19:19-21).

Revelation 19 opens with a heavenly chorus of "a great multitude" singing the praises of God (verse 1). The heavenly choir rejoices with praise because justice has finally been served. "True and righteous are his judgments," they sing, "because He has judged the great harlot" (Revelation 19:2). We then hear a fourfold alleluia:

"Alleluia! Salvation and glory and honor and power belong to the Lord our God" (verse 1).

"Alleluia! Her smoke rises up forever and ever!" (verse 3).

"The twenty-four elders and the four living creatures fell down and worshiped God who sat on the throne, saying, 'Amen! Alleluia!'" (verse 4).

"Alleluia! For the Lord God Omnipotent reigns!" (verse 6).

Christ's Marriage at His Return

The marriage of the Lamb is announced suddenly and dramatically. We have finally arrived at what we have been waiting for all along. The wedding is finally here. John the revelator obviously views this as a future event. The church is the betrothed bride of Christ now, but our marriage to Him is in the future.

This is why we cannot say that the consummation of the marriage has already taken place. The apostle Paul writes, "For I have betrothed you to one husband, that I may present you as a chaste virgin to Christ" (2 Corinthians 11:2). He also writes that Christ "loved the church and gave Himself for her…that He might present her to Himself a glorious church, not having spot or wrinkle or any such thing, but that she should be holy and without blemish" (Ephesians 5:25-27).

The New Testament pictures the church as engaged to Christ at this present time. We are still awaiting the judgment seat of Christ

(2 Corinthians 5:10), presumably after the rapture and before the marriage supper. The marriage ceremony itself will follow in heaven during the Tribulation period on earth.

Revelation 19 pictures Christ symbolically as the Lamb (verse 7), but the picture of the marriage is clearly expressed. The aorist tense of "has come" (Greek, *elthen*) indicates a completed act, showing that the wedding is now consummated. Instead of the normal seven-day Jewish wedding ceremony, this one presumably lasts seven years (during the Tribulation period). The marriage is completed in heaven (Revelation 19:7), but the marriage supper will probably take place later on earth, where Israel is awaiting the return of Christ and the church.

This is the only way to distinguish the bridegroom (Christ), the bride (church), and the ten virgins (Israel) in Matthew 25:1-13. There is no way that He is coming to marry all ten (or five) of these women. They are the attendants (Old Testament saints and Tribulation saints) at the wedding. Only the church is the bride. That is why Jesus could say of John the Baptist that there was not a "greater prophet" (Old Testament saint), but he that is "least in the kingdom of God" (New Testament church) is "greater than he" (Luke 7:28).

The Triumph of Christ's Return

The picture of Christ's return in Revelation 19:11-16 is the most dramatic passage in the entire Bible! In these six verses we are swept up into the triumphal entourage of redeemed saints as they ride in the heavenly procession with the King of kings and Lord of lords. In this one passage alone, all the hopes and dreams of every believer are finally and fully realized. This is not the Palm Sunday procession with the humble Messiah on the donkey colt. This is the ultimate in eschatological drama. The rejected Savior returns in triumph as the rightful King of all the world—and we are with Him.

The description of the triumphant Savior is that of a king leading an army to victory. The passage itself is the final phase of the seventh bowl of judgment begun in Revelation 16:17-21 and moving through the details of 17:1–18:24 and on to chapter 19.

As the scene unfolds, heaven opens to reveal Christ followed by the army of the redeemed. The description of their being clad in white (verse 14) emphasizes the garments of the bride already mentioned earlier (verse 8). In this vignette, the bride appears as the army of the Messiah. But unlike contemporary apocalyptic dramas of that time (such as the War Scroll of the Qumran sect), the victory is won without any military help from the faithful. This army has no weapons, no swords, no shields, no armor. They are merely clad in the "righteous acts of the saints" (verse 8). They have come not to fight, but to watch. They have come not to assist, but to celebrate. The Messiah-King will do the fighting. He alone will win the battle by the power of His spoken word.

The twelvefold description of the coming King combines elements of symbolism from various biblical passages and from the other pictures of the risen Christ in the book of Revelation.

1. He rides the white horse (Revelation 19:11).
2. He is called Faithful and True (Revelation 3:14).
3. He judges and makes war in righteousness (2 Thessalonians 1:7-8).
4. His eyes are as a flame of fire (Revelation 1:14).
5. He wears many crowns (Revelation 4:10).
6. His name is unknown—a wonderful secret (Judges 13:18; Isaiah 9:6).
7. He is clothed in a robe dipped in blood (Isaiah 63:1-6).
8. His name is called The Word of God (John 1:1).
9. A sharp sword is in His mouth (Revelation 19:15).
10. He rules with a rod of iron (Psalm 2:9).
11. He treads the winepress of the wrath of God (Isaiah 63:1-6; Revelation 14:14-20).

12. His written name is King of kings and Lord of lords (Daniel 2:47; Revelation 17:14).

There can be no doubt that this rider on the white horse is Jesus Christ. He comes as the apostle Paul predicted: "in flaming fire taking vengeance on those who do not know God…[who] shall be punished with everlasting destruction…when He comes, in that Day, to be glorified in His saints and to be admired among all those who believe" (2 Thessalonians 1:8-10).

This is the true Christ (the Messiah), not the usurper (the Antichrist). He rides the white horse of conquest, and His victory is sure. His greatness is in the spiritual qualities of His person: He is faithful, true, righteous. His eyes of fire penetrate our sinfulness and expose our spiritual inadequacy. His "many crowns" were probably received from the redeemed, who cast them at His feet in worship (Revelation 4:10). The fact that these crowns are "many" totally upstages the seven crowns of the dragon (Revelation 12:3) and the ten crowns of the beast (Revelation 13:1). His unknown name is a "secret" or "wonder" (see Judges 13:18; Isaiah 9:6). He is Jehovah God Himself—the Yahweh (YHVH) of the Old Testament. He is the I Am whose name is "above every name" (Philippians 2:9).

John wants us to know for certain who this is, so he calls Jesus by his favorite name: The Word (Greek, *logos*) of God (see John 1:1). Christ is the self-disclosure of the Almighty. He is the personal revelation of God to man. He is the personal Word and the author of the written Word. The One revealed is the ultimate revelator of the revelation: Jesus the Christ.

When the Savior returns, He will come from heaven with His bride at His side. The church militant will be the church triumphant. Her days of conflict, rejection, and persecution will be over. She will return victorious with her Warrior-King-Husband.

Every true believer who reads the prediction of Christ's triumphal return in Revelation 19:11-16 should be overwhelmed by its significance. Think about it: We will be in that heavenly army with Him when He returns from glory. In fact, you might want to take a pen and circle the word "armies" in Revelation 19:14 and write your name in the margin next to the verse, for you will be there when He returns!

The destiny of the believer is now fully clarified. Our future hope includes our rapture, Christ's return, and Christ's reign. The church must be raptured to heaven prior to the marriage and prior to her return from heaven with Christ. In the rapture, we will go up to heaven. In the return, we will come back to earth. And in the Millennium, we will reign with Christ on the earth for 1000 years (Revelation 20:4).

The Authority of the King of Kings

In Revelation 19:15 we read this: "Out of His mouth goes a sharp sword, that with it He should strike the nations. And He Himself will rule them with a rod of iron." Christ will come victorious and strike down His enemies. When Christ appears with the heavenly armies, He will not only defeat His enemies (Satan, the Antichrist, and the False Prophet) and the millions they deceive, but also usher in His righteous reign on earth. This fact is seen clearly in the name given to Christ in verse 16: "King of kings and Lord of lords."

A warrior goes into battle with his sword on his thigh, but Christ's sword will be His spoken word. The Word that called the world into being will call human leaders and the armies of all nations to accountability. And Christ Jesus, the living Lord, will be recognized in that day for what He is in reality: King above all kings, Lord above all lords. The prophet Zechariah said it best: "The LORD shall be King over all the earth. In that day it shall be—'The LORD is one,' and His name one" (Zechariah 14:9). Amen!

Lesson 9

The Glorious Appearing

Are you weary from living in a world filled with injustice, pain, and sorrow? Do you tire of struggling with temptation, dealing with difficult people, and enduring society's incessant assaults on that which is godly or biblical? Have you wished Jesus would hasten His return and make all things right?

We trust that is indeed the case with you…that you are among those who live in eager anticipation of the "glorious appearing of our great God and Savior Jesus Christ" (Titus 2:13). After all, as Christians, "our citizenship is in heaven, from which we also eagerly wait for the Savior, the Lord Jesus Christ" (Philippians 3:20). We don't fit in this present world, and as our love for Christ grows, our affection for the world should correspondingly diminish.

The return of Christ will have two phases—the rapture, in which the church is taken up to heaven before the Tribulation, and the return, in which Christ and the church will descend victoriously to the earth. That there are two phases is made evident by at least 15 differences in the descriptions of Christ's coming that cannot be reconciled into one event. (See the chart on pages 53–54.

1. Read Revelation 19:11-16, which provides the most glorious description of Christ's return in all the Bible. Who is the rider on the white horse, and what does He do in verse 11?

2. How is this rider described in verse 12?

3. What name is given to this rider in verse 13?

4. Who follows this rider (verse 14)? What additional light do 1 Thessalonians 3:13 and 4:14 shed on the identity of these followers?

5. What will this rider do, according to Revelation 19:15?

6. What special title is given to this rider in verse 16?

7. With whom will this rider do battle when He returns (verse 19)? What will be the outcome of this encounter (verses 20-21)?

Applying Prophecy to Everyday Life

Are you looking forward to Christ returning to establish His rule on earth? Write two or three reasons you are especially excited about living in this future kingdom.

The Battle of Armageddon

Many people believe we are living in the end times—an era during which the world will be plunged into a series of cataclysmic wars. By the time these wars end, perhaps as much as three-fourths of the earth's population will have died. "Armageddon theology" is the popular designation for Bible prophecies about the end of the world.

In the secular mind, such beliefs are little understood. Some people have even gone so far as to accuse evangelical Christians of trying to hasten the end by advocating a nuclear war as a divine instrument to punish the wicked and complete God's plan for history. These people seem to think that because Christians look forward to the second coming of Christ, they will try to hasten that event.

Yet no right-thinking person wants war, regardless of his views of the end times. We all sense the ominous finality of the predictions about the last days and pray that God will stay His hand of judgment. We may dodge the apocalyptic bullet a few more times, but sooner or later we will have to face the final moment of history.

The Last Battle

Revelation 19 ends with the final triumph of Christ over the Antichrist, presumably at or after the Battle of Armageddon. The passage itself refers to the carnage as the "supper of the great God" (Revelation 19:17). Armageddon is mentioned by name only in Revelation 16:16, but two verses earlier it is called "the battle of that great day of God Almighty" (Revelation 16:14). This includes the pouring of the seventh bowl (Revelation 16:17), the great earthquake (16:18-20), and the fall of Babylon (17:1–19:6).

Armageddon is the final battle of the Tribulation period. A final revolt will occur at the end of the Millennium (Revelation 20:7-10). Armageddon will take place in Israel in conjunction with the second coming of Christ. The battle involves a series of conflicts in and around Jerusalem, as described in Daniel 11:40-45; Joel 3:9-17; Zechariah 14:1-3; and Revelation 16:14-16. It will occur in the final days of the Tribulation when the kings of the world are gathered together for "the battle of that great day of God" (Revelation 16:14).

The site of Armageddon is 50 miles north of Jerusalem in the Valley of Jezreel. This area is also known as the Plain of Esdraelon, near the ruins of the ancient city of Megiddo. The invading army is pictured moving toward Jerusalem from the north and east. The Old Testament prophets all identify Jerusalem as the site where the final phase of the battle will occur.

At Armageddon, the Antichrist, the kings of the earth, and their combined armies will be gathered against Christ and the church to make war. The term "gathered" (Greek, *sunagoge*) in Revelation 19:19 is the same word used in Revelation 16:16 in relation to Armageddon, which tells us the two passages are talking about the same conflict. As we noted earlier, Armageddon may actually be a war of which this is the final battle. The carnage is so extensive that it includes kings, captains, mighty men, cavalry, small men, and great men (19:18).

The prophets predict that God will intervene in human history on behalf of His people and will destroy the Antichrist's army at Jerusalem. Zechariah predicts the battle will end when the Messiah touches down on the Mount of Olives, splits it in half, and enters Jerusalem triumphantly through the Eastern Gate.

What Are the Purposes of Armageddon?

As with many human events, two purposes are at work at Armageddon: a divine intent and a human rationale. The divine purpose is that the judgment at Armageddon prepares for the 1000-year reign of Christ on earth. The satanically inspired human purpose is to once and for all liquidate worldwide Jewry and to establish Satan's control over the entire world.

The Divine Purpose

Our sovereign Lord providentially rules over all history. Thus, all history is the outworking of the decree of the triune God. Nothing takes place that He did not actively plan. All through history, usually unknown to humanity, the battle rages between God and Satan, good and evil. The war of Armageddon is the culmination of a whole series of events that climax in this final act.

According to God's divine purpose, Armageddon will be the venue by which He will judge His enemies. Both satanic and human opposition will be focused on God's elect nation of Israel, and God will bring them to that location to bring down their foolish schemes of rebellion. The psalmist records God's response of laughter at the puny human plans to overthrow God Himself at Armageddon:

> Why do the nations rage,
>   And the people plot a vain thing?
> The kings of the earth set themselves,
>   And the rulers take counsel together,
>   Against the LORD and against His Anointed,
>   saying,

"Let us break Their bonds in pieces
And cast away Their cords from us."

He who sits in the heavens shall laugh;
The Lord shall hold them in derision.
Then He shall speak to them in His wrath,
And distress them in His deep displeasure:
"Yet I have set My King
On My holy hill of Zion" (Psalm 2:1-6).

The Human Purpose

The demented human purpose for the march to Jerusalem appears to be to destroy what these people believe to be the source of the world's problems—the Jews who have now come to faith in Christ. As we follow the buildup to Armageddon in Revelation 11–18, the persecution of Israel begins at the midpoint of the Tribulation, builds, and culminates in the worldwide gathering of armies in Israel.

The Victorious Return

When Christ returns, He will come *with* His church, not to *spare* His church. He will return to spare the human race. He Himself predicted that "unless those days were shortened, no flesh would be saved" (Matthew 24:22). He will return in triumph and win the battle by the power of His spoken word, "the sword…from his mouth" (Revelation 19:21). He will speak, and the battle will be over! Just as He spoke, "Peace, be still!" and the storm ceased (Mark 4:39), so the greatest conflagration in human history will come to an end by His spoken word. He who spoke the worlds into existence will speak again, and the enemy will be slain. The battle will then be over, and Christ and His church will at last be victorious.

Revelation 19 ends with the Antichrist and the False Prophet defeated. Both will be cast alive into the lake of fire. This punishment dramatizes the seriousness of their offense and the finality of Christ's victory over them. The rest of the rebel army will be slain, but they will not be consigned to the lake of fire until the Great White Throne Judgment (Revelation 20:11-15). The fact that the Antichrist and the False Prophet are cast alive into the lake of fire, and that they are still there in Revelation 20:10, indicates that it is a place of eternal, conscious punishment.

In the meantime, Revelation 20:1-2 tells us that Satan will be bound in the bottomless pit for 1000 years before he, too, is cast into the lake of fire. In each case, Christ is the one who sends them into the lake of fire. Jesus alone will determine the final destiny of unbelievers and of the unholy trinity.

As dramatic and climactic as this chapter is, it only sets the stage for the Millennium and the eternal state. The marriage of the Lamb began with the opening ceremonies in heaven. Now the King and His bride will rule for 1000 years on earth. During this time, all of God's promised blessings to Israel will be fulfilled literally as the devastated earth again blossoms like a rose.

Scripture indicates that all the nations of the world will gather for war against Israel. This is a fitting climax to the Tribulation, during which the whole world is in rebellion against heaven (except for a remnant of believers). The Bible teaches that this war will involve not only the whole land of Israel but also all the nations of the world (Zechariah 12:3; 14:2; Revelation 16:14).

Scripture mentions kings (plural) from the east who take a prominent role in the military buildup in preparation for the war of Armageddon. "The sixth angel poured out his bowl on the great river Euphrates, and its water was dried up, so that the way of the kings from the east might be prepared" (Revelation 16:12). The verse may emphasize the Eastern powers simply because that is where the largest masses of population reside. However, we must be careful to observe that the Bible does not name any of these nations. It simply describes them as coming from east of the Euphrates, which could also refer to Muslim nations there.

When we consider that the whole Tribulation will be a war between God and His opponents—Satan, the fallen angels, the Antichrist, the False Prophet, and the rest of unregenerate mankind—we should not be surprised that it will include a great number of military conflicts. The biblical data lead us to believe that the Tribulation will be a time of great military conflict—so much so that we can consider the entire Tribulation period as a world war.

What Are the Stages of Armageddon?

A detailed study of all the biblical passages pertaining to Armageddon reveals a very complex campaign. One of the most thorough studies of the campaign is by Arnold Fruchtenbaum, who has divided the campaign into eight stages.[1] Although other plans can just as readily be proposed, his evaluation seems to us to be the most logical and comprehensive.

> The two climactic events of the Great Tribulation are the Campaign of Armageddon and the second coming of Jesus Christ. A considerable amount of data is given about this time period in the Scriptures. One of the greatest difficulties in the study of eschatology is placing these events in chronological sequence in order to see what exactly will happen in the Campaign of Armageddon...The Campaign of Armageddon can be divided into eight stages, and this in turn will facilitate an understanding of the sequence of events.[2]

Each of these eight stages serves a distinct purpose in the overall campaign. Although no single biblical passage provides a sequence of all the events, this plan seems to put all the pieces together in the most coherent and comprehensive way.

1. The assembling of the allies of the Antichrist (Psalm 2:1-6; Joel 3:9-11; Revelation 16:12-16).

2. The destruction of Babylon (Isaiah 13–14; Jeremiah 50–51; Revelation 17–18).

3. The fall of Jerusalem (Micah 4:11–5:1; Zechariah 12–14).

4. The armies of the Antichrist at Bozrah (Jeremiah 49:13-14).

5. The national regeneration of Israel (Psalm 79:1-13; 80:1-19; Isaiah 64:1-12; Hosea 6:1-3; Joel 2:28-32; Zechariah 12:10; 13:7-9; Romans 11:25-27).

6. The second coming of Jesus Christ (Isaiah 34:1-7; 63:1-3; Habakkuk 3:3; Micah 2:12-13).

7. The battle from Bozrah to the Valley of Jehoshaphat (Jeremiah 49:20-22; Joel 3:12-13; Zechariah 14:12-15).

8. The victory ascent on the Mount of Olives (Joel 3:14-17; Zechariah 14:3-5; Matthew 24:29-31; Revelation 16:17-21; 19:11-21).

Stage 1: The Antichrist's Allies Assemble

The primary biblical reference to this first stage is Revelation 16:12-16, where the Euphrates River is dried up to prepare the way for "the kings of the east," culminating at Armageddon. The assembling of the armies begins at the same time as the divine judgment of the sixth bowl. At this time the Euphrates River will be dried up, providing for a faster and easier assembly of the armies of the kings from the east. In the Bible, "east" refers to the region of Mesopotamia (Assyria and Babylon), which today includes Islamic nations such as Iraq, Iran, Afghanistan, Pakistan, and the former Soviet "stans." The drying up of the Euphrates River will allow the forces of the Antichrist to assemble out of Babylon, his capital. The armies joining him will be those of the seven remaining kings out of ten described in Daniel 7:24-27 and Revelation 17:12-13. Their goal will be the final destruction of the Jews.

Stage 2: Babylon Is Destroyed

In this stage the focus shifts from the gathering armies of the Antichrist to the destruction of Babylon, which is his capital, by opposing forces. While the Antichrist is away with his armies at Armageddon, his capital will be attacked and destroyed. The irony is that while the Antichrist is gathering his armies in northern Israel for the purpose of attacking God's city (Jerusalem), God attacks the Antichrist's city (Babylon). In the Old Testament, Babylon was the place of Israel's captivity as well as the originating site of idolatry. Known also as Shinar (Genesis 10:10; 11:2; Daniel 1:2; Zechariah 5:11), Babylon will be a worldwide economic and religious center of activity during the Tribulation (Revelation 17–18). Whether one interprets "Babylon" literally or figuratively, the end result of its judgment will be decisive and devastating.

According to Isaiah 13:19 and Jeremiah 50:40, the destruction will be as devastating and complete as was that of Sodom and Gomorrah. Once the attack and destruction are finished, Babylon will be uninhabitable and will never again be rebuilt (Revelation 18:21-24). The Antichrist will be a world ruler, but his control will not be so absolute as to preclude rebellion or to squelch all opposition (Daniel 11:41). He will try, but these things will be tactically impossible. The destruction of Babylon will come as divine punishment for its long history of antagonism and evil against the people of Israel, and the result will be the razing of the city.

> "I will repay Babylon and all the inhabitants of Chaldea for all the evil they have done in Zion in your sight," says the LORD. "Behold, I am against you, O destroying mountain, who destroys the whole earth," says the LORD, "and I will stretch out My hand against you, roll

you down from the rocks, and make you a burnt mountain. They shall not take from you a stone for a corner nor a stone for a foundation, but you shall be desolate forever," says the LORD (Jeremiah 51:24-26).

Stage 3: Jerusalem Falls

Although the Antichrist's capital will have been destroyed in the second phase of the campaign, his forces will not have been lost. Rather than moving eastward to confront the attackers of his capital, the Antichrist will move south against Jerusalem.

> The burden of the word of the LORD against Israel... "Behold, I will make Jerusalem a cup of drunkenness to all the surrounding peoples, when they lay siege against Judah and Jerusalem. And it shall happen in that day that I will make Jerusalem a very heavy stone for all peoples; all who would heave it away will surely be cut in pieces, though all the nations of the earth are gathered against it" (Zechariah 12:1-3; see also 14:1-2).

The Antichrist's forces will sweep down to Jerusalem, and once again the city will fall into Gentile control. Although Zechariah 12:4-9 and Micah 4:11–5:1 describe a temporary resurgence of Jewish strength and stiff resistance, Jerusalem will fall. The losses on both sides will be enormous, but the Antichrist's forces will prevail. With the fall of Jerusalem, the campaign's third stage will come to an end.

Stage 4: The Antichrist Moves South Against the Remnant

In the fourth stage, the campaign will shift into the desert and mountains, probably to the area of Bozrah and Petra, about 80 miles south of Jerusalem. At the beginning of the second half of the Tribulation, after the Antichrist breaks his treaty with Israel (Daniel 9:27;

Matthew 24:15), many of the Jews will flee into the desert for safety. This will fulfill the words and exhortation of Jesus in Matthew 24:16-31. In verse 16, Jesus says of those who see the abomination of desolation, "Then let those who are in Judea flee to the mountains." This flight for life is also described in Revelation 12:6,14.

After Jerusalem is captured, the Antichrist will move south in an attempt to destroy those who fled in the previous three and a half years. In Micah 2:12 we read of God's gathering and protection of this remnant: "I will surely assemble all of you, Jacob, I will surely gather the remnant of Israel; I will put them together like sheep of the fold, like a flock in the midst of their pasture."

The area normally associated with this part of the campaign is that of Mount Seir, about 30 miles south of the lower end of the Dead Sea. Two sites are possibilities for the location of the fleeing Jews, Bozrah and Petra (see Isaiah 33:13-16 and Jeremiah 49:13-14). As the forces gather in the rugged wilderness of Mount Seir, the fourth phase will come to an end, and the last few days of the campaign will begin.

Stage 5: The Regeneration of the Nation Israel

The campaign of Armageddon will culminate in the second coming of Christ. But before Christ returns, Israel will confess its national sin (Leviticus 26:40-42; Jeremiah 3:11-18; Hosea 5:15) and plead for the Messiah to return (Isaiah 64:1-12; Zechariah 12:10; Matthew 23:37-39). This will come as the armies of the Antichrist gather to destroy the Jews in the wilderness. According to Hosea 6:1-3, the Jewish leaders will issue a call for the nation to repent. The nation will respond positively and repent for two days.

> The leaders of Israel will finally recognize the reason why the Tribulation has fallen on them. Whether this will be done by the study of the Scriptures, or by the preaching of the 144,000 or via the Two Witnesses or by the ministry of Elijah, is not clearly stated. Most likely there will be

a combination of these things. But the leaders will come to a realization of the national sin in some way. Just as the Jewish leaders once led the nation to the rejection of the Messiahship of Jesus, they will then lead the nation to the acceptance of His Messiahship by issuing the call of Hosea 6:1-3, which will begin the last three days before the Second Coming.[3]

The fifth stage will come to completion on the third day of Israel's confession and prayer for Messiah's return. In the sixth stage, God, having heard their prayers, will answer them, fulfilling biblical prophecy and the hope of the ages.

Stage 6: The Second Coming of Jesus Christ

In the sixth stage the prayers of the Jews are answered, and Jesus Christ will return to earth to defeat the armies of the Antichrist at Bozrah and to begin the final portions of the campaign. He will return to earth in the clouds, in the same manner in which He departed (Matthew 24:30; Acts 1:9-11). The fact that Jesus returns first to the mountain wilderness of Bozrah is seen in Isaiah 34:1-7; 63:1-6; Micah 2:12-13; and Habakkuk 3:3. At His second coming, Jesus Christ the Messiah will enter battle against the Antichrist's forces and miraculously defeat them.

According to Jude 14-15 and Revelation 19:11-16, Jesus will return with an angelic army and with the church saints (robed in white at the marriage of the Lamb) who had been raptured prior to the Tribulation. Revelation 19:11-16 makes it clear that the second coming will bring destruction to the enemies of Jesus Christ. These verses describe Him as treading the winepress of the wrath of God and ruling with a rod of iron.

At Israel's request, Jesus Christ will return to earth and enter the battle against the Antichrist and his armies. He will save the Jews in the wilderness from destruction and will then continue to Jerusalem to save the remnant there and conclude the campaign (Zechariah 12:7).

Stage 7: The Final Battle

In the seventh phase, Jesus the Messiah will fight alone on Israel's behalf, destroying the Antichrist and those who have come against the nation and persecuted it. In this phase the Antichrist will be slain by the true Christ. Among the very first casualties will be the Antichrist himself. Having ruled the world with great power and spoken against the true Son of God, the counterfeit son will be powerless before Christ. Habakkuk 3:13 says, "You went forth for the salvation of Your people, for salvation with Your anointed. You struck the head from the house of the wicked, by laying bare from foundation to neck." Second Thessalonians 2:8 tells us, "The lawless one will be revealed, whom the Lord will consume with the breath of His mouth and destroy with the brightness of His coming."

Beginning at Bozrah and moving back to Jerusalem and the Kidron Valley, also known as the Valley of Jehoshaphat, Jesus will engage and destroy the Antichrist's forces (Joel 3:12-13; Zechariah 14:12-15; Revelation 14:19-20). In the Valley of Jehoshaphat, along the eastern walls of Jerusalem, the nations and armies that gathered against the Jews to destroy them will now find themselves being destroyed by Jesus Christ, the Messiah and King of the Jews.

Stage 8: The Ascent to the Mount of Olives

With the destruction of the Antichrist and his forces complete, the campaign will be over, and Jesus will stand on the Mount of Olives in a symbolic victory ascent. When He does so, a number of cataclysmic events will occur, bringing the Tribulation to an end.

> Then the LORD will go forth and fight against those nations, as He fights in the day of battle. And in that day His feet will stand on the Mount of Olives, which faces

Jerusalem on the east. And the Mount of Olives shall be split in two, from east to west, making a very large valley; half of the mountain shall move toward the north and half of it toward the south (Zechariah 14:3-4).

Then the seventh angel poured out his bowl into the air; and a loud voice came out of the temple of heaven, from the throne, saying, "It is done!" And there were noises and thunderings and lightnings; and there was a great earthquake as had not occurred since men were on the earth. Now the great city was divided into three parts, and the cities of the nations fell (Revelation 16:17-19).

The supernatural calamities that come upon the world at this time correspond to the seventh bowl judgment and include the greatest earthquake the world has ever known. As a result of the earthquake, Jerusalem will split into three areas, and the Mount of Olives will split into two parts, creating a valley and means of escape from the earthquake for the Jewish inhabitants of the city.

When Will This Happen?

The Old Testament prophets predicted that the Messiah will come to deliver Israel when the nations repent and turn to the one "whom they pierced" (Zechariah 12:10). In response to their prayers, Christ will return to deliver Israel from the clutches of the Antichrist. He will return bodily and literally, just as He departed in His ascension to heaven.

Every biblical text that deals with Christ's triumphant return emphasizes the great victory He will win at that time. For example, the apostle Paul wrote, "Then the lawless one will be revealed, whom the Lord will consume with the breath of His mouth and destroy with the brightness of His coming" (2 Thessalonians 2:8).

The Battle of Armageddon ends with Christ proclaiming victory over the Antichrist, the False Prophet, and the devil. Revelation 19:20 declares that the Antichrist and the False Prophet will both be captured and "cast alive into the lake of fire." Revelation 20:2-3 adds that Satan will be bound in the abyss, or bottomless pit, for 1000 years. During this time, Satan will be inactive and thus unable to deceive the nations any longer.

What Happens After Armageddon?

Armageddon will be the last great world war of the Tribulation period, and it will take place in Israel in conjunction with the second coming of Christ. The Bible is clear that it is a certain and cataclysmic event yet to come. According to the Bible, great armies from the east and the west will gather and assemble to strike a final blow against Israel.

There will be threats to the power of the Antichrist from the south, and he will also move to the east before finally turning his forces toward Jerusalem to subdue and destroy it. As he and his armies move against Jerusalem, God will intervene, and Jesus Christ will return to rescue His people Israel. The Lord and His angelic army will destroy the armies, capture the Antichrist and the False Prophet, and cast them into the lake of fire (Revelation 19:11-21).

In a sense, Armageddon is a battle that never really takes place—at least not in accordance with its original human intent. Its human purpose will be to gather the armies of the world to execute the Antichrist's final solution to the "Jewish problem." This is why Jesus Christ chooses this moment in history for His return to earth—to thwart the Antichrist's attempted annihilation of the Jews and to destroy the armies of the world.

God's purpose in allowing the Tribulation is to bring about the conversion of Israel and multitudes of Gentiles (Revelation 7:4-14). But once the Antichrist attempts to wipe them out, the final wrath of God's judgment will fall at Armageddon. Still, in the heat of battle there is a great note of hope and triumph. Jesus Christ will win the victory, vanquish the enemy, and establish His kingdom on earth.

So the Battle of Armageddon will bring the Tribulation to an end and usher in 1000 years of peace and blessing through the reign of Christ on earth. During this time, all of God's prophetic promises to Israel will finally be fulfilled, and Christ will reign in peace on David's throne.

Lesson 10

The Battle of Armageddon

The word "Armageddon" has Hebrew roots. *Har* means "mountain" or "hill," and *Magedon* is a reference to the ruins of an ancient city that overlooks the Valley of Esdraelon in northern Israel. In the Battle of Armageddon, the leaders of the world, headed by Antichrist, will gather their armies to fight against the nation of Israel. Through the ages, Satan has longed to eradicate Israel because he wants to prevent God's promises from being fulfilled through His chosen people.

The Battle of Armageddon will be Satan's last attempt, and as always, he will not succeed. As 1 Kings 8:56 says, "There has not failed one word of all [God's] good promise." Up to today, God's track record for fulfilling His promises stands at 100 percent, and there is absolutely nothing Satan can do to change the outcome of the prophecies that have not yet been fulfilled.

1. Briefly describe the scene in Revelation 16:12. Why does this happen?

2. Whom do the spirits of demons gather together in verse 14?

3. Where does this gathering take place (verse 16)?

---

4. What scene does Zechariah 14:2-3 describe for us in Jerusalem?

5. What will the Lord do in response (verses 8-9)?

6. According to Zechariah 12:10 and Romans 11:26-27, what miracle will take place?

7. During the battle, where will Christ make His victorious descent (see Zechariah 14:4)?

8. How does Matthew 24:29-31 describe Christ's return? Who will witness this event?

―∞∞∞―

Applying Prophecy to Everyday Life

In the Battle of Armageddon, the Antichrist's forces will be so massive and daunting, the situation will appear to be hopeless. But when Jesus returns, the Antichrist's defeat will be instant and complete. God is still in full control of all that happens. He who brought about the perfect fulfillment of every single one of the prophecies of Christ's first coming will also bring about the perfect fulfillment of every single one of the prophecies of Christ's second coming.

What level of comfort and encouragement does this give you in light of the steadily worsening evil in our world?

11

THE MILLENNIAL KINGDOM

The Old and New Testaments contain numerous references to the kingdom of Christ, the long-anticipated time when the Lord Jesus Himself will reign on the earth. This is, in fact, one of the more frequently mentioned subjects in the Bible. Many names are used to describe this period, including the kingdom age, the age of peace, the reign of Christ, and the Millennium. Not to be confused with the eternal realm of heaven, this temporary kingdom will be a time of peace on earth, which mankind has always yearned for.

Throughout the centuries, every scheme devised by man to forge a utopian world has failed. Why? There are two reasons. First, man has a sinful and degenerate heart and cannot produce a world of peace, regardless of how hard he tries. Second, as long as Satan is roaming free on the earth, there will always be war. He is not only a deceiver but also a hater of men, and he continues to pit nations against each other. The proliferation of war even in this era of the United Nations is evidence that man will always fail in his attempts to secure peace. The United Nations was established to help bring about a permanent discontinuation of war. However, since its inception, there have been more wars and more bloodshed than in any comparable period of world history.

When Jesus taught His followers to pray, "Thy kingdom come" (Matthew 6:10 KJV), He was referring specifically to the millennial kingdom. It will certainly be the most incredible kingdom in all of human history—a kingdom in which Jesus, the anointed King, will have the nations for His inheritance (Psalm 2:8), when "the wolf also shall dwell with the lamb" (Isaiah 11:6), and "the earth shall be full of the knowledge of the LORD" (Isaiah 11:9).

Just how long will this kingdom last? Only one chapter in the Bible reveals this information—Revelation 20. There, the phrase "thousand years" is mentioned six times in the first seven verses. For example, verse 6 says, "Blessed and holy is he who has part in the first resurrection. Over such the second death has no power, but they shall be priests of God and of Christ, and shall reign with Him a thousand years."

Understanding the Millennium

The word "millennium" is a Latin term that means "a thousand years." Despite the many biblical references to the millennial reign of Christ, and despite the fact that Christians will play a vital role in it, most believers know very little about this critical period in our planet's future. Before we find out more about this kingdom, let's first examine the three major views people have held historically regarding the millennial kingdom.

Premillennialism is the belief that the second coming of Christ to set up His earthly kingdom will occur prior to the millennial age. This is the view accepted by nearly all Bible scholars who take the Scriptures literally and at face value whenever possible.

There are others who believe the world is going to become more and more "Christianized" in time and, as a result, usher in the kingdom of Christ on its own merits. In this scenario, Jesus would return at the end of the Millennium to an already-righteous earth. This belief is known as *postmillennialism*. A third viewpoint, known as *amillennialism*, holds to a nonliteral or spiritualized interpretation of Scripture and attempts to allegorically explain away the coming Millennium. In the amillennial scheme, there is no anticipation of a literal reign of Christ on earth.

The early Christians were unquestionably premillennialists. In fact, the disciples and those whom they taught anticipated the return of Christ and the establishment of His kingdom on earth in their lifetime. There are detractors of the premillennial view who claim that it is a relatively new theory, but the truth is that premillennialism was the dominant view held during the first three centuries of the early church.

Premillennialists believe that the rapture, the Tribulation, and the glorious appearing of Christ will all occur before the beginning of the Millennium. During this time, Satan will be bound for 1000 years, and a theocratic kingdom of peace on earth will ensue with Jesus as its King. According to Revelation 20, the righteous will have already been raised from the dead prior to the Millennium (at the rapture) and will participate with Christ in the reign of His kingdom.

Confusion About the Millennium

Toward the end of the third century AD, the allegorizing of Scripture began to consume theological ideology. Philosophy replaced the study of Scripture, and premillennialism, along with many other important biblical teachings (such as salvation by grace), fell into disrepute. Not until after the Reformation of the sixteenth century was there a revival of premillennial thought. As the twentieth century began to unfold, Bible institutes and Christian colleges sprang up across America emphasizing a solid, literal interpretation of the Bible, and with them, a return to premillennialism. Today, despite continued attacks, premillennialism remains the most dominant perspective of the three millennial views among evangelicals.

Amillennialism holds that there will be no literal kingdom on the earth following the second coming of Christ. It tends to spiritualize and allegorize all prophecies concerning the Millennium, and yet-to-be-fulfilled prophecies relating to Israel are attributed to the church instead. Amillennialists also believe Satan was bound during Christ's first appearance on earth 2000 years ago, an argument that can hardly be substantiated when one considers the present condition of our world and Peter's observation that "the devil walks about like a roaring lion" (1 Peter 5:8).

Furthermore, amillennialists aren't sure whether the Millennium is being fulfilled currently on earth or whether it's being fulfilled by the saints in heaven. However, they tend to agree that our current state of affairs is probably as good as the world is going to get and that the eternal realm, not the millennial kingdom, will immediately follow the second coming of Christ. Those who hold to this view go to great lengths to avoid the simple and plain literal interpretation of Scripture regarding the binding of Satan and the reign of Christ for 1000 years on earth (Revelation 20:2-7).

Postmillennialism is the belief that the world will continue to get better and better until the entire world is christianized, at which time Christ will return to a kingdom already flourishing in peace. Although this view was popular at the beginning of the twentieth century, it has all but died out as a result of the World Wars, the Great Depression, and the overwhelming escalation of moral evil in our society. Those of the preterist persuasion are making a concerted attempt to resuscitate the postmillennial theory but are not gaining much headway, primarily because most laypeople who read the Bible tend to take it literally. And if one takes Bible prophecy literally, it becomes apparent that the world will continue to get worse, not better, prior to the Millennium.

The Millennial Kingdom

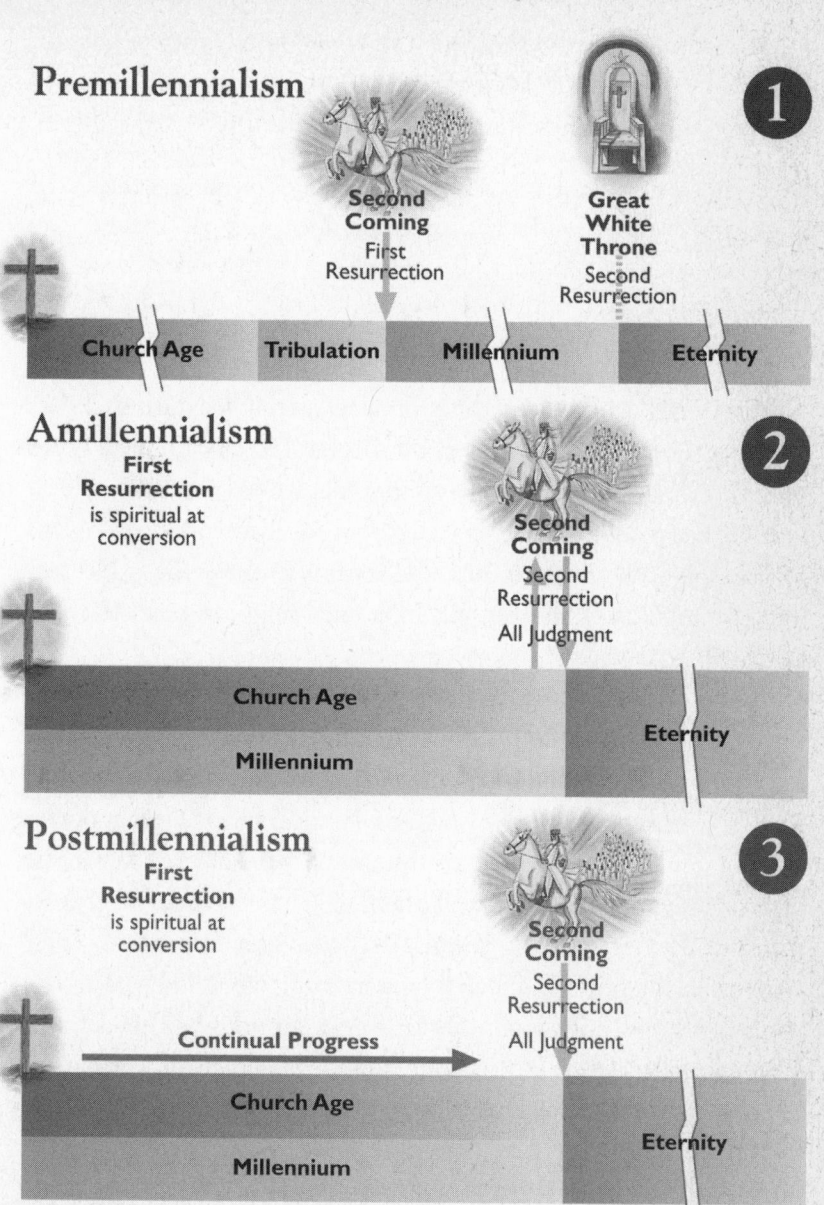

Premillennialism ①

Second Coming
First Resurrection

Great White Throne
Second Resurrection

| Church Age | Tribulation | Millennium | Eternity |

Amillennialism ②

First Resurrection
is spiritual at conversion

Second Coming
Second Resurrection
All Judgment

Church Age
Millennium
Eternity

Postmillennialism ③

First Resurrection
is spiritual at conversion

Second Coming
Second Resurrection
All Judgment

Continual Progress

Church Age
Millennium
Eternity

Excerpted and adapted from Tim LaHaye and Thomas Ice, *Charting the End Times* (Eugene, OR: Harvest House Publishers, 2001), p. 129.

The Premillennial Hope

According to the premillennial view, the rapture of the church, followed by the Tribulation and the glorious appearing of Jesus, will take place prior to Christ's establishment of His 1000-year kingdom.

> Unto us a Child is born, unto us a Son is given; and the government will be upon His shoulder. And His name will be called Wonderful, Counselor, Mighty God, Everlasting Father, Prince of Peace. Of the increase of His government and peace there will be no end (Isaiah 9:6-7).

Although the first part of this prophecy was fulfilled during Christ's first appearance on earth, the second part has yet to be fulfilled. At no time was the government on Jesus' shoulder when He was here 2000 years ago, nor has there ever been a global government of peace. This kingdom will occur when our Lord returns to the earth at His second coming and establishes His millennial reign on earth (Revelation 5:10).

Many of the one-world government advocates today believe that the only hope for world peace in our time is to have a world dictator. From a biblical standpoint, no mere human being is competent to fill such a position. History has proven time and again that power corrupts and absolute power corrupts absolutely. If a man were to be given the role of world dictator (which will, in fact, occur for a short time during the horrifying Tribulation period that immediately precedes the Millennium), inevitably everything would fall apart. The earth requires a holy, loving, merciful leader who will treat mankind equitably. Jesus Christ alone qualifies for that role, and until He comes, the world will never know true peace.

How Will the Millennial Kingdom Begin?

After the last of the judgments at the conclusion of the seven-year Tribulation, the Lord will appear in the sky for all to see. He will be accompanied by the angels and by His bride, the church. "Behold, He is coming with clouds, and every eye will see Him, even they who pierced Him. And all the tribes of the earth will mourn because of Him" (Revelation 1:7).

The glorious appearing of Jesus Christ in the clouds will signal the beginning of the millennial era. At this point, the Battle of Armageddon will end, the Antichrist will be cast into the lake of fire, and Satan will be bound for the duration of the 1000-year kingdom. Jesus will also divide the remaining survivors of the Tribulation into two groups.

> When the Son of Man comes in His glory, and all the holy angels with Him, then He will sit on the throne of His glory. All the nations will be gathered before Him, and He will separate them one from another, as a shepherd divides his sheep from the goats. And He will set the sheep on His right hand, but the goats on the left. Then the King will say to those on His right hand, "Come, you blessed of My Father, inherit the kingdom prepared for you from the foundation of the world" (Matthew 25:31-34).

The "goats" mentioned here are the millions of unsaved and unbelieving followers of the Antichrist who will take the mark of the beast, persecute the Jews, and kill the Christians during the Tribulation. They will immediately be cast into hell. The "sheep" are those Gentiles who will refuse to take the mark and will befriend and protect the Jews during this period. These surviving Jews and Gentiles will enter the millennial kingdom in their natural bodies and repopulate the earth during the 1000 years of Christ's rule.

Another group of people will also occupy the earth during the Millennium—those with immortal, resurrected bodies. This includes everyone who received a new body at the rapture and the Tribulation saints who were resurrected at the appearance of Christ. It is quite probable that it will also include Gentile believers who Jesus said will "sit down with Abraham, Isaac, and Jacob in the kingdom" (Matthew 8:11). This group will not procreate but will rule and reign with Christ during this period of time. Only those who exist in their natural bodies will be able to procreate.

During the Millennium, Jesus, the holy Judge, will reign supreme. His kingdom will be one of righteousness. Satan will be bound for the duration, so there will be no deception (although at the end of the Millennium, Satan will be briefly released before being bound for eternity). This era will be a time of global peace without any fear of fellow man. It will also be a time of longevity. People's lifespans will increase dramatically; consequently, the earth's population could reach unprecedented numbers, most of whom will be believers in Christ.

One of the characteristics of our present time is that so few people really know about God and the Bible. But during the Millennium, it won't be necessary to preach the gospel anymore because those who dwell on the earth will know it.

> I will put My law in their minds, and write it on their hearts; and I will be their God, and they shall be My people. No more shall every man teach his neighbor, and every man his brother, saying, "Know the LORD," for they all shall know Me, from the least of them to the greatest of them, says the LORD. For I will forgive their iniquity, and their sin I will remember no more (Jeremiah 31:33-34).

The coming 1000-year kingdom will be the most incredible era ever in earth's history. It will be a time of unprecedented peace, when those who have accepted Jesus Christ as their Lord and Savior will be able to rule and reign along with their loving King. It will most certainly be a time best described by the word *utopia*.

> They shall beat their swords into plowshares, and their spears into pruning hooks; nation shall not lift up sword

against nation, neither shall they learn war anymore (Isaiah 2:4).

Such world peace is beyond finite human comprehension. There is no way depraved humanity will ever be able to bring about such conditions on earth. But, thank God, such will be reality when Jesus returns to reign on the earth.

A Wondrous Age

From the time of the fall of Adam and Eve in the Garden of Eden, humanity and creation have suffered God's judgment and the consequences of their original sin. The pollution of sin has affected all of humanity and all of creation. The apostle Paul reminds us of that which we experience daily when he declares in Romans 8:22, "We know that the whole creation has been groaning as in the pains of childbirth right up to the present time" (NIV). However, during the 1000-year millennial kingdom, there will be a partial lifting of the curse and the consequences of original sin. There will still be death (for those who entered the Millennium in their natural bodies), and the complete effects of the fall will not be lifted until the creation of the new heaven and new earth in the eternal state after the Millennium (Revelation 22:3).

The coming literal kingdom of Christ to this earth will be the most blessed time this world has known since the Garden of Eden. In fact, many Edenic features will characterize it. All those who rebelled against God will be gone. Satan will be bound so he cannot tempt man, and Christ will enforce righteousness with the help of His holy angels and the church. Pornographers, criminals, and others who corrupt society will no longer be able to ply their evil trades.

The coming kingdom will bring unprecedented prosperity, and everyone will have his own home. The curse on the earth will be lifted, and the ground will bear incredible harvests. Cheating and war will be nonexistent, so people will be able to enjoy the fruits of their labors.

Longevity will be increased to almost what it was prior to the flood, when people lived nearly 1000 years. At least that will be the case for believers, who will live from the time of their birth until the end of the kingdom. Isaiah 65:20 indicates that a person will be considered still a child at 100.

Not only will lifespans be considerably longer in the millennial kingdom, but the world population will be enormous. Jeremiah 33:22 speaks of this large population: "As the host of heaven cannot be numbered, nor the sand of the sea measured, so will I multiply the descendants of David My servant and the Levites who minister to Me." In Zechariah 8:5 we read that "the streets of the city shall be full of boys and girls," proving that the population in Israel will increase dramatically. Keep in mind that we will live under ideal conditions in the millennial kingdom—there will be no wars to wipe out large numbers of people, and we will not experience the level of violence seen now or during the Tribulation period.

A Time of Faith

The millennial kingdom will be a time of faith, when the majority of the population will become believers. We see that in several Bible passages. Christ will be in charge, so people's minds won't be blinded to the gospel by immoral media programming. Body-damaging substances will not be available, so people will not have their minds fogged from the truths of Scripture. Satan will be bound so he cannot blind people's spiritual eyes. Art forms will glorify Christ during the millennial kingdom. Jeremiah 31:31-34 indicates that everyone will be so acquainted with the gospel that no one will need to share it with his neighbor.

The government and politics of the millennial kingdom will focus on the benevolent reign of Jesus Christ as Israel's Messiah-King. It will be a theocracy centered in Jerusalem (Isaiah 2:1-4), where Jesus will reign as Messiah and King of Israel, thus fulfilling God's prophetic promise to King David in the Davidic covenant (2 Samuel 7:12-16). God's covenant with David guaranteed that David's dynasty, throne, and kingdom would continue forever. When Jesus Christ returns at the end of the Tribulation, He will reestablish the Davidic throne in His personal rule (Jeremiah 23:5-8). Other significant passages describing Christ's reign over Israel include Psalm 2; Isaiah 9:6-7; Jeremiah 33:20-26; Ezekiel 34:23-25 and 37:23-24; and Luke 1:32-33. These and other Bible passages provide ample evidence that the kingdom promised to David will be fully realized in the future.

A Rebellious Youth Movement

But in spite of all the ideal conditions arranged by God to attract a maximum number of people to accept His free gift of salvation by receiving His Son, many will rebel at the end of the 1000-year kingdom. Revelation 20 indicates that at the end of the 1000 years, Satan will be loosed from the bottomless pit to "go out to deceive the nations"—that is, to tempt them to rebel against God. God allows this to happen so that all the unsaved people living on the earth will be forced to decide whether they will receive Christ before God establishes the eternal order.

Sadly, even after living for almost 1000 years under the righteous reign of Christ, a multitude "whose number is as the sand of the sea" (Revelation 20:8) will nonetheless rebel against God when given the opportunity. People rebel because of their own will. Satan's appearance on the scene at this point will simply bring to the surface the rebellion in the hearts of those who "are not willing to come" to Him that they might have eternal life (John 5:40).

The End of Satan

Revelation 20:10 says, "The devil, who deceived them, was cast into the lake of fire and brimstone where the beast and the false prophet are. And they will be tormented day and night forever and ever." Living creatures will suffer indefinitely in the lake of fire. Two men—the Beast (the Antichrist) and the False Prophet—will be thrown into the lake of fire at the beginning of the 1000-year kingdom (Revelation 19:20), yet they are spoken of in the present tense in Revelation 20:10, indicating that they are still there. It is into this lake of fire that Satan will be cast. He, the Antichrist, the False Prophet, and all those from every age in history who rejected God's free offer of salvation through faith in Christ "will be tormented day and night forever and ever." The Bible clearly states that this punishment will last for all eternity!

Lesson 11

The Millennial Kingdom

After the Tribulation, the Lord Jesus Christ will reign on the earth for 1000 years, after which He will then usher us into eternity. During this 1000-year kingdom, humanity will get a taste of what it's like to live under God's rule rather than man's. From the time of the fall of humanity, people have tried time and again to bring about true and lasting peace, but no one has succeeded. Regardless of how hard we try, we are destined for failure because we are all fallen creatures.

In the millennial kingdom, however, we will know perfect justice and peace. Society will not be directed by the fickle whims of men, but by our all-knowing and ever-faithful Savior. We will literally experience heaven on earth!

1. On pages 144-147, three different views of the millennial kingdom are presented. Name each view and describe it in a sentence or two.

2. Revelation 20:1-6 provides for us some details about the millennial kingdom. Who will be bound at the beginning of Christ's 1000-year reign, where will he be bound, and for how long?

3. Briefly describe how the world will be a different place when Satan is bound (see Isaiah 2:4 and Jeremiah 31:33-34).

4. Read Revelation 20:4 and Revelation 6:9-11. Who will be among those who reign with Christ during the millennial kingdom?

5. Revelation 20:6 mentions the "first resurrection," that is, the people who populate the millennial kingdom. According to 1 Corinthians 15:23 and 1 Thessalonians 4:13-18, who will be among those in the first resurrection?

6. What will happen at the end of the millennial kingdom, according to Revelation 20:7-10?

7. Where will Satan, the Antichrist, and False Prophet receive their punishment (see Revelation 20:10)? For how long?

Applying Prophecy to Everyday Life

Christ's rule on earth is still a future event, but if you're a Christian, He lives and rules in your heart right now. Are you living in a way that acknowledges His kingship? In what ways can you grow more in this area?

12

THE GREAT WHITE THRONE JUDGMENT

One of the most sobering passages in the Bible is Revelation 20:11-15. Here, unbelievers are given a glimpse of what their eventual encounter with God will be like. This passage describes the Great White Throne Judgment. This fearsome event will occur at the end of Christ's 1000-year reign. In fact, it is the last event scheduled before we enter the age of the new heaven and new earth as outlined in Revelation 21–22.

The great statesman Daniel Webster was once asked, "What is the greatest thought that has ever passed through your mind?" Webster instantly replied, "My accountability to God." Nowhere is man's accountability to his Creator more clearly presented than in this particular section of Scripture.

> I saw a great white throne and Him who sat on it, from whose face the earth and the heaven fled away. And there was found no place for them. And I saw the dead, small and great, standing before God, and books were opened. And another book was opened, which is the Book of Life. And the dead were judged according to their works,

by the things which were written in the books. The sea gave up the dead who were in it, and Death and Hades delivered up the dead who were in them. And they were judged, each one according to his works. Then Death and Hades were cast into the lake of fire. This is the second death. And anyone not found written in the Book of Life was cast into the lake of fire (Revelation 20:11-15).

The Bible makes it abundantly clear in a number of passages that judgment for all people will most certainly follow death. For example, Hebrews 9:27 says, "It is appointed for men to die once, but after this the judgment." This verse not only disputes the pagan concept of reincarnation but also suggests that everyone will eventually be judged. Unfortunately, most people try not to think about that while they are alive. And the criteria by which we are judged will be determined by our status in Christ. Believers and unbelievers will be judged at different times and in very different ways.

The People Who Will Be Judged

Judgment of Believers

Immediately following the rapture (before the Tribulation, Millennium, and Great White Throne Judgment), believers will stand before the judgment seat of Christ in heaven as described in 2 Corinthians 5:10. Here, the resurrected saints will receive rewards for the good works they performed while on earth. According to 1 Corinthians 3:11-15, bad works will be "burned," as will good works performed with wrong motives:

No other foundation can anyone lay than that which is laid, which is Jesus Christ. Now if anyone builds on this foundation with gold, silver, precious stones, wood, hay, straw, each one's work will become clear; for the Day will declare it, because it will be revealed by fire; and the fire will test each one's work, of what sort it is. If anyone's work which he has built on it endures, he will receive a reward. If anyone's work is burned, he will suffer loss; but he himself will be saved, yet so as through fire.

Note that at no time is any believer's salvation in jeopardy. Simple faith in Jesus Christ guarantees a believer's place in heaven. His good works, however, will determine his status in heaven. Appearing before the judgment seat of Christ will be a time of indescribable joy for those who faithfully served Jesus Christ while on earth.

Judgment of Unbelievers

That is a far cry from what will happen to the unbelievers sentenced to appear before the Great White Throne at the end of the Millennium. No believer in Jesus will be judged at the Great White Throne Judgment—only unbelievers.

On a flight from Salt Lake City to San Francisco, I (Tim) was seated next to a salesman who claimed he had never read a Bible. The closest he had ever been to a church was to drop off his daughter every other week for Sunday school on his way to the golf course. I asked him if he would submit to an experiment, and he agreed. Many people say the Bible is a difficult book to understand, particularly the book of Revelation. Turning to Revelation 20:11-15, I handed him my Bible with only this brief instruction: "This is a prophecy about a future event." I waited as he read. His cheerful mood changed abruptly, and so he exclaimed, "If that's true, I'd better get right with God!"

That salesman put into words the main reasons God has given us so much information about the afterlife judgment that awaits all those who reject or neglect God. He does not want people to face eternity in hell. He longs for people to become saved and live with Him forever in heaven. Acts 17:30-31 explains that God will judge the world by "the Man whom He has ordained." We may well ask, whom has He ordained? The answer appears in the latter part of the verse: "He has given assurance of this to all by raising Him from the dead." The Lord Jesus Christ is the only Person in world history who can match this description. He is the only One who could judge the world in righteousness, for only He is without sin (1 Peter 2:22).

Revelation 20:12 describes those at the Great White Throne Judgment as the "dead, small and great." These people, regardless of their stature or position, died without acknowledging and accepting Jesus Christ's payment for their sins. Whether in the earth or sea, a grave or mausoleum, the ashes or remains of the deceased will one day be raised and united with their souls so they can stand before the Great White Throne.

During this judgment, books will be opened that contain the records of every deed and thought (including those performed in secret) of every unbeliever. "God will bring every work into judgment, including every secret thing, whether good or evil" (Ecclesiastes 12:14).

Apparently God has prepared a complete set of books that reveal everything about a person's life. These books will be opened on judgment day. It's a little unnerving to think that each of us may have a recording angel following us around, tabulating our every word or deed. The actions and intentions of those who have foolishly chosen not to have their sins erased by the sacrifice of Jesus will be judged according to the law of the Old Testament. As Galatians 3:10 reveals, those who live under the law, and not under Christ, will be judged by the law. Unless we accept God's mercy through His Son, we cannot be found righteous, "for all have sinned and fall short of the glory of God" (Romans 3:23).

The Criteria of Judgment

Hebrews 2:2 tells us that "every transgression and disobedience receive[s] a just reward." This is consistent with the justice of God and seems to indicate that there will be different levels of punishment in hell. A relatively moral citizen, such as a doctor, teacher, or nice old neighbor who has lived a comparatively good life (though short of the standard of God) would not be subjected to the same punishment as someone such as Adolph Hitler, whose regime murdered millions of God's chosen people. Likewise, those heathen who never heard the gospel will be judged accordingly and certainly far less severely than those who heard the gospel message repeatedly and rejected it. In Matthew 11:21-24, Jesus explains that the people who heard His message and rejected it would be subjected to greater condemnation than the sinners who lived in the cities of Sodom and Gomorrah.

The Great White Throne Judgment is for unbelievers, who will be judged by the standards of God's law. During this judgment, the Book of Life will be opened just to make sure of a person's eternal status. If a person's name does not appear in the Book of Life (he wouldn't be there if it did), he will be cast into the lake of fire for all eternity. This checking of the Book of Life serves to highlight God's mercy. No one will be unjustly condemned. Second Peter 3:9 states, "The Lord is…not willing that any should perish but that all should come to repentance." When Jesus died on the cross, He took upon Himself the sins of every person, both past and future. God desires that all accept His gift of salvation, but unfortunately, multitudes through the ages have chosen instead to ignore this free gift and consequently have lost their opportunity for eternal life with Him.

Revelation 3:5 indicates believers can never be blotted out from the Book of Life. Revelation 21:27 tells us that the only people who will enter the Holy City (heaven) are "those who are written in the Lamb's Book of Life." It is therefore essential that one have his or her name written in this book if he or she wants to go to heaven.

The Identity of the Judge

Who is the Judge who will be sitting on the Great White Throne? Acts 17:31 indicates it is the One who was raised from the dead.

John 5:22 tells us, "The Father judges no one, but has committed all judgment to the Son." Thus, Jesus Christ Himself will sit on the Great White Throne. As Hebrews 4:13 says, "All things are naked and open to the eyes of Him to whom we must give account." It will be a sobering day indeed for those who find themselves standing before the very Judge whom they have mocked, rejected, ignored, or cursed. On that day, all will wish they had accepted His free gift of salvation, but by then it will be too late to do so.

People who have elected to ignore the countless advantages of a relationship with Christ, including His free gift of eternal life, often provide well-worn excuses in order to somehow validate their neglect of spiritual matters. One such excuse can be phrased like this: "I'm not interested in learning about a God who demonstrates His cruelty by sending people to hell." Of course, such a statement is based on a lack of knowledge. As Scripture clearly indicates, our God is a merciful God who has gone to tremendous lengths in order to rescue His creation.

In a sense, those who end up in hell will go there because ultimately they prefer it to the alternative of spending eternity in heaven. Such a statement might surprise you, but consider this: What was the first thing Adam and Eve did when they sinned? They tried to hide from their all-knowing Creator. Why? Because once they had sinned, they couldn't stand to be in His holy presence.

Those who accept Jesus' payment for their sins at some point during their life will be free from the penalty of their sins and, upon entering heaven in their new bodies, will be able to fellowship with their Creator. By contrast, those who refuse to accept Jesus as their Lord and Savior will still possess their sins when they die. Theoretically, then, they would feel extremely uncomfortable in heaven, to put it mildly. They would feel the same way Adam and Eve felt in God's presence after they fell.

The Various Books of Judgment

"Books were opened…And the dead were judged according to their works, by the things which were written in the books" (Revelation 20:12). Evidently God owns a complete set of books that records every thought, motive, and action of a person's life, waiting to be recalled on judgment day. Each of us may have an angel who, in this life, is responsible for recording everything we do. In connection with this thought, we do well to consider Ecclesiastes 12:14: "God will bring every work into judgment, including every secret thing, whether good or evil." In this final hour, the books of each person's works (his or her deeds) will be opened.

The Bible indicates that both believers and unbelievers will be judged by their works to determine either their rewards or the degree of their punishment. As we have already seen, believers will receive their rewards at the judgment seat of Christ (2 Corinthians 5:10). Unbelievers will be judged at the Great White Throne Judgment (Revelation 20:11-16). The books (plural) will be opened at this judgment to determine the severity of their punishment. Anyone whose name is recorded in the Book of Life will be eternally saved. But Revelation 20:15 says, "Anyone not found written in the Book of Life was cast into the lake of fire."

The New Testament refers to the Book of Life eight times, and although the Old Testament does not call it by that name, it does allude three times to a book in which names are written. The psalmist says that the righteous have their names written in "the book of the living" (Psalm 69:28), so it is a book in which righteous people have their names written, indicating their eternal salvation.

One Last Event

An awesome scene is described in Philippians 2:9-11 that is rarely mentioned in relation to the future judgment, but it should be. The apostle Paul wrote this about Jesus:

> God also has highly exalted Him and given Him the name which is above every name, that at the name of Jesus every knee should bow, of those in heaven, and of those on earth, and of those under the earth, and that every tongue should confess that Jesus Christ is Lord, to the glory of God the Father.

After giving a wonderful description of how Christ was willing to humble Himself and become "obedient to the point of death, even the death of the cross" (verse 8), Paul warns that a day is coming when "every knee should bow" and "every tongue should confess that Jesus Christ is Lord." All the skeptics and all those who reject Christ will acknowledge that Jesus Christ is Lord! Believers won't be the only ones who bow and acknowledge Christ as Lord. However, their final acknowledgment of the lordship of Christ will come too late for their salvation.

Because all people will one day bend their knee to Jesus Christ—and this will probably happen at the close of the Great White Throne Judgment—it is far better to acknowledge Christ as Lord now, voluntarily, rather than to reject Him in this life and wait to be forced to do so that day and then be cast into the lake of fire.

An Abundance of Warnings

One reason God has given us so much information in His Word about the judgment that awaits those who reject or neglect Him is that He doesn't want anyone to face eternity in hell. His desire is for everyone to choose salvation and thereby live with Him forever in heaven. Jesus Himself warned, "Most assuredly, I say to you, unless one is born again, he cannot see the kingdom of God" (John 3:3).

Unless people are born again (born anew from above) and have their sins erased, they will not be prepared for the spiritual delights of heaven. What's more, heaven cannot be contaminated by sin. Heaven would cease to be heaven if sin were to enter into it. Christians are fit for heaven not because they are good or because they deserve it, but because they choose to accept God's pardon for their sins and the cleansing power of Christ's death on the cross. Those who do not make this choice will not be fit for heaven.

During this life, we are all confronted with a choice. We can admit we are sinners in need of a Savior and invite Jesus into our lives, or we can reject Him. Where we spend eternity will be determined by that choice. If you have not made a decision for Christ, please do so before it's too late.

Lesson 12

The Great White Throne Judgment

Christians can look forward to the future with great anticipation because they have the promise of heaven. But not unbelievers. For them, the future is one big unknown. And the warning that they will one day face judgment should bring great trepidation to their hearts.

Unfortunately, there's a common misperception that everyone will be judged at one time—both Christians and unbelievers. But in actuality, God's children will face a judgment related not to their salvation, but to rewards based on their works on earth. And unbelievers will face the Great White Throne Judgment, which is the final judgment for all people of all ages who rejected God during their time here on earth.

So that we might better distinguish between the two judgments, let's look at them more carefully.

The Judgment of Christians

1. Read 1 Corinthians 3:10-15. Who is the foundation upon which Christians build (verses 10-11)?
2. What different kinds of building material will Christians use (verse 12)?
3. What will the fire in verse 13 be used for?
4. What will happen if a person's works endure? If his or her works don't endure?

The Judgment of Unbelievers

1. Read Revelation 20:11-15. What scene is described in verse 12?
2. Will anyone be able to escape this judgment (see verse 13)?
3. What are these people judged according to (see verses 12b and 13b)?
4. What will happen to those whose names are not found in the Book of Life (verse 15)?
5. What can we learn from Matthew 25:41 and Mark 9:43-44 about the lake of fire?
6. How long will this punishment last (see Matthew 25:41,46)?
7. What does Luke 16:26 say about those who are in heaven or hell?

Applying Prophecy to Everyday Life

As Hebrews 9:27 says, "It is appointed for men to die once, but after this the judgment." In other words, there is no second chance. Are you certain about your eternal destination? If not, see pages 175-176 and learn how to trust Christ as your personal Savior. And if you are a Christian, we trust that the sober reality of future judgment burdens your heart to share the good news of Jesus Christ with friends and family members who are unbelievers.

13

Heaven and Eternal Life

The concept of life after death is not unique to Christianity and is, in fact, the universal dream of mankind. It is so integrated into the human psyche that nearly every religion has been built on this expectation. Opinions, philosophies, and religions may differ, but very few people consider death to be the end of life. From the primitive tribesmen of the jungles to the sophisticated mystics of the East, virtually every tradition has some system of belief regarding the afterlife. Even some of those who have attempted suicide have confessed that their ultimate rationale was to find a better set of circumstances in the next life.

Why do most people hold to this belief in life after death? Could it be intuitive? Did God place this thought within us? If so, we expect the Bible to reveal truthful insights about it. Indeed, Christianity tells without a doubt the most beautiful story of the afterlife—for believers. The Bible provides far more believable details about the next life than any other so-called holy book. That should come as no surprise to Christians, who believe the source of the Bible to be the Creator Himself.

The foundation of Christianity is the resurrection of Jesus Christ. The Lord provided His own resurrection as the paramount sign of His deity. Although Jesus' disciples were a defeated group following His crucifixion, they were subsequently motivated to world evangelism following His resurrection. As Luke documented in the first chapter of Acts, "He...presented Himself alive after His suffering by many infallible proofs." The Christian belief in life after death is based on the fact of Christ's resurrection.

The Promise of Eternal Life

Jesus promised His followers, "Because I live, you will live also" (John 14:19). Not surprisingly, no one in the Bible speaks more about the resurrection than Jesus Christ Himself. In John 11:25-26, for example, He said, "I am the resurrection and the life. He who believes in Me, though he may die, he shall live. And whoever lives and believes in Me shall never die." Jesus was saying that although those who believe in Him may die physically, the real person, which is the soul and spirit, will never die.

> Most assuredly, I say to you, he who hears My word and believes in Him who sent Me has everlasting life, and shall not come into judgment, but has passed from death into life. Most assuredly, I say to you, the hour is coming, and now is, when the dead will hear the voice of the Son of God; and those who hear will live. For as the Father has life in Himself, so He has granted the Son to have life in Himself, and has given Him authority to execute judgment also, because He is the Son of Man. Do not marvel at this; for the hour is coming in which all who are in the graves will hear His voice and come forth—those who have done good, to the resurrection of life, and those

who have done evil, to the resurrection of condemnation (John 5:24-29).

This passage assures us that both the righteous and unrighteous will be resurrected. Eternal life is therefore guaranteed for all. However, where and how that future will play out depends entirely on one's position in Christ.

Our Eternal Destiny

Prior to the death, burial, and resurrection of Jesus Christ, all people who died were taken to a place known as Sheol or Hades. Speculated to be located at the center of the earth, this place had two compartments separated by a large chasm or gulf. The first section was known as "paradise," the "place of comfort," or "Abraham's bosom." This is where the Old Testament saints would go following death. On the other side of the great gulf was the "place of torment," where those who died without faith were held (see Luke 16:26). From the time of Jesus' resurrection, believers have not gone to the "place of comfort" in Sheol. Rather, they have been instantly transported to heaven to be with the Lord (see 2 Corinthians 5:8). Unbelievers, on the other hand, are still taken to the "place of torment" in Sheol/Hades.

The word *heaven* appears nearly 600 times in the Bible. It can refer to three different places: 1) the sky, 2) outer space, or 3) the third heaven, which Paul speaks of in 2 Corinthians 12. This third heaven is where God dwells with His angels and His people. This is where believers who have died are today. Everything that is truly precious to us as Christians will be in this third heaven, including the triune God, our loved ones who are believers, our inheritance, our citizenship, and our eternal rewards. In other words, everything of eternal value will be there.

When the rapture occurs, we who are believers will instantly receive our new, immortal, resurrected bodies. At the rapture, Christ will come to take us home to the Father's house in heaven (John 14:1-4). Many of us look forward to that glorious day when we will see the unfathomable magnificence of heaven, be reunited with loved ones, and come face-to-face with Jesus, our Savior.

However, some of us fail to realize that immediately following the rapture, we will stand before the judgment seat of Christ and receive rewards, if any, for the good works we performed in the name of Christ during our time on earth. Then, while still in heaven, we will participate in the marriage of the Lamb, where we will become the bride of Christ (Revelation 19:7-9). Finally, after the Tribulation (which will take place while we believers are in heaven), we will return with Jesus to earth and rule with Him during the 1000-year kingdom (Revelation 20:1-3).

The bodies of those who happen to be alive on earth at the time of the rapture, along with the bodies of believers who have already died, will be changed from corruptible into incorruptible (see 1 Corinthians 15:52-54). Presently, our bodies are unfit for heaven and must be transformed into bodies similar to Christ's resurrection body. These new, resurrected bodies (made from the elements of our old bodies gathered together by the Lord) will be recognizable, able to communicate, and able to eat, just as Jesus ate with His disciples after His resurrection (see Luke 24:41-43; John 21:9-14). Jesus demonstrated that He could walk through walls and travel great distances at the speed of thought in His resurrected body. We will be able to do the same. In our new, sinless, immortal bodies, we will rule and reign with Christ throughout the Millennium. Afterward, we will enter the new heaven for all eternity.

The Eternal State

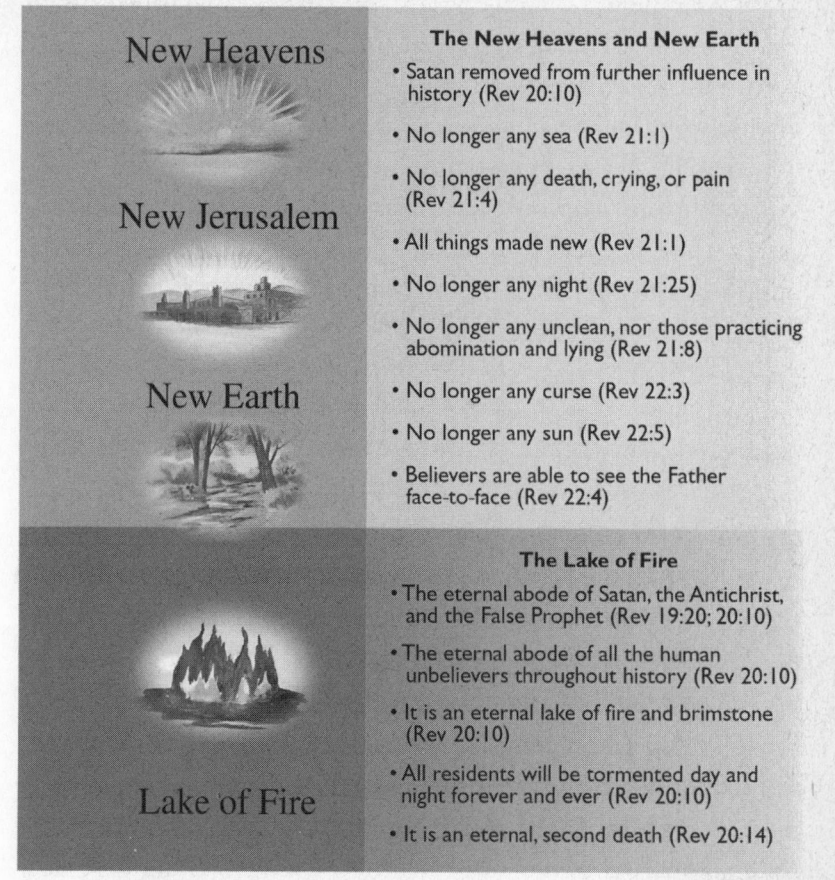

New Heavens

New Jerusalem

New Earth

The New Heavens and New Earth

- Satan removed from further influence in history (Rev 20:10)

- No longer any sea (Rev 21:1)

- No longer any death, crying, or pain (Rev 21:4)

- All things made new (Rev 21:1)

- No longer any night (Rev 21:25)

- No longer any unclean, nor those practicing abomination and lying (Rev 21:8)

- No longer any curse (Rev 22:3)

- No longer any sun (Rev 22:5)

- Believers are able to see the Father face-to-face (Rev 22:4)

Lake of Fire

The Lake of Fire

- The eternal abode of Satan, the Antichrist, and the False Prophet (Rev 19:20; 20:10)

- The eternal abode of all the human unbelievers throughout history (Rev 20:10)

- It is an eternal lake of fire and brimstone (Rev 20:10)

- All residents will be tormented day and night forever and ever (Rev 20:10)

- It is an eternal, second death (Rev 20:14)

Excerpted and adapted from Tim LaHaye and Thomas Ice, *Charting the End Times* (Eugene, OR: Harvest House Publishers, 2001), p. 76.

Eternal Punishment of the Lost

Contrasting sharply with the glorious future that awaits each and every believer, the fate of the unbeliever is simply too horrifying to even imagine. As mentioned earlier, at the moment of death, the unbeliever is instantly taken to the place of torment in hell (Greek, *Hades*). According to Revelation 20:11-15, at the conclusion of the millennial kingdom, unbelievers will be resurrected and brought out of Sheol/Hades to stand before Jesus Christ at the Great White Throne Judgment. There, they will be judged "according to their works" (verse 13) using the law of the Old Testament. None have been born again, and their names do not appear in the Book of Life, so none will be able to enter the kingdom of God. All these unbelievers will then be cast into the lake of fire, where they will be tormented for all eternity. Had they accepted Christ's free gift of salvation while they were alive on earth, they would not have had to be punished with eternal separation from God.

The term "lake of fire" appears five times in Revelation (19:20; 20:10,14-15; 21:8). It is a place of conscious punishment. At present, no one is in the lake of fire. Its first occupants will be the Beast and the False Prophet (Revelation 19:20). When unbelievers die today, they go immediately to hell (Hades) to await their final trial at the Great White Throne Judgment. After that they will be condemned to the lake of fire for all eternity. Those cast into the lake of fire will experience "the second death" (Revelation 21:8). The first death is physical death, whereas the second involves eternal punishment.

The place of torment is certainly a place of punishment. But it serves only as a holding place for those awaiting trial. By contrast, the lake of fire is a place of permanent incarceration from which there is no release. In the New Testament, this place serves as a symbol of eternal punishment (see Matthew 25:41-46; Mark 9:44-48).

No Other Options

Despite the teachings of many in today's world, we must be clear that God's Word does not allow for other options regarding the afterlife. Purgatory is said to be the place where people go to do penance or suffer for the sins they have committed in this world in order to purify them for a better afterlife. The startling difference between the biblical presentation of the present state of the dead and this false teaching is that the Bible indicates that those in "the place of torment" will spend eternity in the lake of fire, and those in heaven will spend 1000 years in the millennial kingdom and then be in the new heaven and earth for all eternity. There are no places in between and no other options. Luke 16:26 makes clear that anyone who goes to the place of torment can never bridge the great gulf and enter paradise. On the contrary, all those who are presently in torment will eventually be cast into the lake of fire.

The suggestion that those in torment today will be granted a later opportunity to be saved contradicts Isaiah 38:18, which says, "Sheol cannot thank You, death cannot praise You; those who go down to the pit cannot hope for Your truth." The place of torment is a place of suffering and is void of the teaching of truth. Therefore those who enter that place cannot hope for escape. This is a tragic truth, and we cannot diminish its reality in any way.

The Bible makes it clear that there are only two ultimate destinies—heaven or hell. There is no clear teaching in Scripture to indicate intermediate places such as limbo or purgatory. These concepts were created by human imagination and were never included in divine revelation. Nor does the Bible teach such ideas as an unconscious intermediate state such as "soul sleep" or a second chance for salvation for those who are already in eternal punishment.

New Heaven and New Earth

At the conclusion of Christ's 1000-year millennial reign on earth and the Great White Throne Judgment, the Bible describes the formation of "a new heaven and a new earth" (Revelation 21:1), of which the New Jerusalem, a city of indescribable beauty, will be the capitol. That there will be a major overhaul of the universe appears to have been part of God's plan all along, for it was promised through the Old Testament prophets.

Behold, I create new heavens and a new earth; and the

former shall not be remembered or come to mind. But be glad and rejoice forever in what I create; for behold, I create Jerusalem as a rejoicing, and her people a joy. I will rejoice in Jerusalem, and joy in My people; the voice of weeping shall no longer be heard in her, nor the voice of crying (Isaiah 65:17-19).

The last two chapters of the Bible describe the New Jerusalem in some detail, a magnificent eternal dwelling place for God and His people.

Now I saw a new heaven and a new earth, for the first heaven and the first earth had passed away. Also there was no more sea. Then I, John, saw the holy city, New Jerusalem, coming down out of heaven from God, prepared as a bride adorned for her husband. And I heard a loud voice from heaven saying, "Behold, the tabernacle of God is with men, and He will dwell with them, and they shall be His people. God Himself will be with them and be their God. And God will wipe away every tear from their eyes; there shall be no more death, nor sorrow, nor crying. There shall be no more pain, for the former things have passed away" (Revelation 21:1-4).

John goes on to describe the scene in heaven. The New Jerusalem is the abode of the saved of all time: Old Testament saints, New Testament believers, and the Tribulation and millennial saints alike. The entire redeemed family of God will live together there for all eternity. The gates are named for the 12 tribes of Israel, and the jeweled foundations for the 12 apostles (21:12-14). There will be no Temple in the New Jerusalem because God Almighty is there. And there will be no sun because the glory of God will fill the eternal city.

In essence, it will be "paradise regained." The river of life and the tree of life will be there (22:1-2). The curse of the law will be eradicated by the blood of the Lamb, and we will reign with Christ "forever and ever" (22:5). It is no wonder that the hope of heaven has always been the longing of every true believer.

You Must Decide

Keep in mind that all of us are sinners from birth. Those who spend eternity in heaven will do so only because they accepted Christ's payment for their sins while they were alive on the earth. Those who end up in hell for all eternity will do so because they died without receiving Jesus as their Savior. Jesus Himself clearly explained how to obtain admittance into heaven when He said, "I am the way, and the truth, and the life. No one comes to the Father except through Me" (John 14:6).

Only through Jesus Christ can we gain access to the Father, who is in heaven. Romans 3:23 says "all have sinned and fall short," and Romans 6:23 says "the wages of sin is death." Only through faith in the Lord Jesus Christ and His work on the cross can we escape. There is no other way and no second chance. "As many as received Him, to them He gave the right to become children of God, to those who believe in His name" (John 1:12).

Have you put your faith in Jesus Christ for what He did for you on the cross? Until you say yes, you can have no hope of spending eternity in heaven. You won't get there by doing the best you can. That will never be good enough. You can only get to heaven by believing that Jesus alone paid for your sins. He alone is good enough to get you to heaven. He did everything necessary to secure your salvation when He died for your sins on the cross. And it's up to you to decide whether He meant what He said when He promised, "He who believes in the Son has everlasting life" (John 3:36) and "The one who comes to Me I will by no means cast out" (John 6:37).

In the Bible, God invites you to trust Jesus Christ as your personal Savior. Scripture says, "If you confess with your mouth the

Lord Jesus and believe in your heart that God has raised Him from the dead, you will be saved…For 'whoever calls on the name of the LORD shall be saved'" (Romans 10:9,13). If you have not done this yet, why not call on Him right now? Express your faith and trust in Him by praying something like this:

> *God, I know that I have sinned against You and that I need Your forgiveness. I do believe with all my heart that Jesus died on the cross for my sins and that He rose from the dead, conquering sin. I am trusting Jesus alone to forgive my sins, save my soul, and give me eternal life. Right now I take Him as my personal Savior and place all my faith and trust in Him. I am praying this in Jesus' name. Amen.*

Lesson 13

Heaven and Eternal Life

In the last two chapters of the Bible, God pulls back the curtain and gives us a glimpse of heaven. And what an incredible scene we see! The description of our future home is rich with details, and yet this is just a tiny preview of what's to come. Mere words are inadequate to describe what God has prepared for us in eternity.

1. With whom will we dwell in heaven (Revelation 21:3)?
2. What "former things" will have passed away (verse 4)?
3. What is the extent of our inheritance (verse 7)?
4. What will the New Jerusalem be made out of (verse 18)?
5. What does verse 23 tell us about our future home?
6. What will never enter this city (verse 27)?
7. To what tree will we have access once again (Revelation 22:2)?
8. What will be our occupation (22:3)?
9. How long will we reign alongside God (22:5)?

———— ∞∞∞ ————

Applying Prophecy to Everyday Living

What do you look forward to most about heaven? How can you allow that to positively impact the way you are living today on earth?

A Final Word: Until He Comes

The timing of the last days is in God's hands. From a human standpoint, it appears that we are standing on the threshold of the final frontier. The pieces of the puzzle are all in place. As the sands of time slip through the hourglass of eternity, we are all moving closer to an appointment with destiny. The question we all should be asking is, how much time is left?

The tension between dealing with today and anticipating tomorrow is one of the difficult realities of living the Christian life. We often find ourselves caught between the here and now and the hereafter. On the one hand, we need to be ready for Jesus to come at any moment. On the other hand, we have God-given responsibilities to fulfill in this world right now.

We are living in a time of great crisis, but it is also a time of great opportunity. We must be prepared for the challenges that lie ahead of us. New technologies will make our lives more convenient, but they will also make us more dependent on those conveniences. Medical advancements will continue to pose enormous challenges in the area of bioethics. The shifting sands of sociopolitical change will also challenge our national and international policies in the days ahead. We will find ourselves living in a very different world from the one into which we were born. All of these changes and challenges will confront us in the days ahead.

Preparing for Christ's return is something each one of us must do for ourselves. No one else can get our hearts ready to meet God. That's our own responsibility. Jesus urges us to do three things in view of His second coming:

1. Keep watching (Matthew 24:42).
2. Be ready (Matthew 24:44).
3. Keep serving (Matthew 24:46).

Erwin Lutzer, the senior pastor of Moody Church in Chicago, has highlighted "five unshakable pillars" that enable us to live with eternity in view.[1]

1. God still reigns.

Human leaders will come and go. Some will be better, some worse. Some will be what we deserve—a reflection of our own weakness and sinfulness. But behind the scene of human governments, God reigns over the eternal destiny of mankind. Beyond this temporal world, God rules from the throne in heaven. He guides His children and overrules in the affairs of men and nations to accomplish His will and purposes. The Bible assures us, "There is no authority except that which God has established" (Romans 13:1 NIV). Regardless of who our leaders are, we are to offer "prayers, intercession and thanksgiving...for kings and all those in authority" (1 Timothy 2:1-2 NIV).

2. The church is still precious.

During this present age, God is still working through His church to evangelize the world. Jesus gave us clear direction about what we are to be doing until He returns. "Go and make disciples of all nations, baptizing them in the name of the Father and of the Son and of the Holy Spirit, and teaching them to obey everything I have commanded you. And surely I am with you always, to the very end of the age" (Matthew 28:19-20 NIV). The church may flourish or be persecuted in the days ahead, but we are to be faithful to our mission until Jesus calls us home to glory (1 Thessalonians 4:13-17).

3. Our mission is still clear.

The church stands as the salt and light of God in society. "You are a chosen people, a royal priesthood, a holy nation, God's special possession, that you may declare the praises of him who called you out of darkness into his wonderful light" (1 Peter 2:9 NIV). Lutzer suggests that we can accomplish this by 1) representing Christ to the world by a godly lifestyle, 2) winning people to Christ through intellectual and moral confrontation with a loving persuasiveness, and 3) strengthening our families as a testimony to God's grace. The integrity of sincere and authentic Christian lives and families speaks volumes to a lost world that is desperate for meaning and purpose. We cannot underestimate the spiritual impact that true Christianity has on those who have no answers to the overwhelming problems of life. When Christians live out their faith with authenticity and boldness, they capture the attention of the watching world.[2]

4. Our focus is still heaven.

Modern American Christians can easily forget that heaven is our real destiny. So many believers today live in such peace and affluence that they forget about heaven. We actually think that God's purpose is to bless our lives here on earth. Dave Hunt has observed, "Unfortunately, too many persons—even dedicated Christians—find heaven a topic of only minor interest because they consider it irrelevant to the challenges of this present life."[3] We must remember, however, that this world is no friend to grace. As time passes, we should expect a continual moral decline in secular society. The Bible reminds us that there will be an "increase of wickedness" and that "terrible times" will come in the last days (Matthew 24:12 NIV; 2 Timothy 3:1 NIV). In the meantime, whatever success we have in this world must be measured in the light of our eternal destiny. Joe Stowell reminds us that making heaven our primary point of reference will transform our relationship to everything that is temporary in this world.[4] C.S. Lewis wrote, "Christians who did most for the present world were just those who thought most of the next."[5]

5. Our victory is still certain.

The ultimate Bible prophecies focus on the triumph of Christ and His bride—the church (Revelation 19). They assure us that we will share in His victorious reign. Whatever transpires in the meantime must be viewed in light of our eternal destiny. Peter Marshall, former chaplain of the US Senate, said, "It is better to fail at a cause that will ultimately succeed than to succeed in a cause that will ultimately fail."[6] Until the trumpet sounds and the Lord calls us home, we have the Great Commission to fulfill and the world to evangelize. There is no reason to let up now. We have no clear date for the termination of the present age, so we must keep on serving Christ until He comes.

A young African martyr wrote these words in his prison cell before he died:

> I'm part of the fellowship of the unashamed. The die has been cast, I have stepped over the line, the decision has been made. I'm a disciple of Jesus Christ. I won't look back, let up, slow down, back away or be still.
>
> My past is redeemed, my present makes sense, my future is secure. I'm finished and done with low living, sight walking, smooth knees, colorless dreams, tamed visions, worldly talking, cheap giving and dwarfed goals.

My face is set, my gait is fast, my goal is heaven, my road is narrow, my way is rough, my companions are few, my guide is reliable, my mission is clear. I won't give up, shut up, let up until I have stayed up, stored up, prayed up for the cause of Jesus Christ.

I must go till He comes, give till I drop, preach till everyone knows, work till He stops me. And when He comes for His own, He will have no trouble recognizing me because my banner will have been clear.[7]

Jesus gave His disciples the Great Commission, telling them they would be empowered by the Holy Spirit to be His witnesses in Jerusalem, Judea, Samaria, and "to the end of the earth" (Acts 1:8). Then, to their amazement, He ascended into heaven, leaving them gazing intently into the sky. Two men in white (probably angels) appeared and asked, "Why do you stand gazing up into heaven? This same Jesus, who was taken up from you into heaven, will so come in like manner as you saw Him go into heaven" (verse 11).

All too often, today's Christians are just like those early disciples. We spend more time gazing into the sky and speculating about Christ's return than we do serving Him. The point the angels were making to the disciples is that Jesus' return is certain. Thus we shouldn't waste time and energy worrying about when or whether Christ will return. Believe that He is coming again, on schedule, and stay focused on doing His business in the meantime.

Jesus left several instructions about what we should do while we await His return:

1. *Witness for Him everywhere you go.* Our Lord told His disciples to be His witnesses everywhere—even to the end of the earth (Acts 1:8).

2. *"Go into all the world and preach the gospel"* (Mark 16:15). This command emphasizes the evangelistic and

missionary nature of the church's ministry during the present era. We are to take the gospel to the whole world.

3. *"Repentance and remission of sins should be preached in His name to all nations"* (Luke 24:47). We're to call men and women to repent and believe the gospel.

4. *"Make disciples of all the nations, baptizing them"* (Matthew 28:19). Making converts and discipling them in their walk with God is a major emphasis of the church's mission.

5. *Continue building the church in every generation.* Jesus told His disciples that He would build His church with such power that "the gates of hell shall not prevail against it" (Matthew 16:18 KJV). Jesus pictured the church being on the march until He calls us home.

6. *"Occupy till I come"* (Luke 19:13 KJV). In the parable of the talents, the servants were to put their master's money to work until the master returned. We are to stay busy about the Master's business until He returns.

7. *Remain faithful until He returns.* Our Lord concluded His prophetic Olivet Discourse by reminding His disciples to continue in faithful and wise service even though He might be gone a long time (Matthew 24:45; 25:14-30).

That Final Day

The world is speeding toward its ultimate destiny. Every day that passes moves us closer to the end. The people and the planet have a divine appointment to keep. As the clock of time ticks away, mankind comes closer and closer to earth's final hour.

It is only a matter of time until our planet will be plunged into the most devastating catastrophe imaginable. The outcome is certain and is clearly predicted in biblical prophecy. The only real question is, how much time is left?

Almost 2000 years ago, the apostle Peter said, "The end of all things is near. Therefore be alert and of sober mind so that you may pray" (1 Peter 4:7 NIV). Way back in the New Testament era, Peter and the other apostles sensed that they had moved dramatically closer to the consummation of God's plan for this world. The Old Testament age had come to an end, and they were now part of a new era.

Peter's reference to the end is expressed by a perfect-tense verb in the Greek text. This means the action involved is a present reality with future consequences. It could just as appropriately be translated, "The end of all things has already begun." For Peter, the end of the age was already a present reality.

The first coming of Christ initiated the end of the age (see Acts 2:14-20; Hebrews 1:2), and His second coming will terminate the end of the age (Matthew 24:30). Therefore, the last days include the entire church age.

Scripture also speaks of the end as a future event. The apostle Paul predicted, "There will be terrible times in the last days" (2 Timothy 3:1 NIV). The Apocalypse reveals "what must soon take place" (Revelation 1:1 NIV) and warns us that "the time is near" (verse 3). Scripture also presents Christ's coming as an imminent reality. He promised, "Behold, I am coming quickly!" (Revelation 22:7). He will come suddenly, and He could come at any moment.

That leaves us asking, what time is it now? Peter referred to the *present*, saying, "[Christ] was revealed in these last times" (1 Peter 1:20 NIV). At the same time, Peter referred to the coming of Christ as a future event, "ready to be revealed in the last time" (1 Peter 1:5). It is clear that he viewed the last times as both a present reality and a future event.

The Bible affirms three basic facts about the coming of Christ at the end of the age.

We are living in the last days. Every generation of Christians has lived with the hope of the imminent return of Christ. We believe that He could return at any moment. There is no prophetic event that remains to be fulfilled before the way can be opened for Him to return. In fact, certain events, like the return of Israel to its land, indicate that we are close to the end.

God's timetable is not our timetable. Peter himself told us that "scoffers will come in the last days," questioning the promise of His second coming (2 Peter 3:3-4). They will reject the idea of God's intervention in human history and suggest that all things are moving forward at their own pace without God. These skeptics will also fail to anticipate God's coming judgment on the world (2 Peter 3:8). God's perspective is not limited to human time. But we dare not mistake the patience of God for a change in His plans. He is waiting, giving His people time to repent. The Bible warns, "He who is coming will come and will not delay" (Hebrews 10:37 NIV).

Christ's coming is always growing closer. The Bible emphatically promises that Christ is coming again (Luke 12:40; Philippians 3:20; Titus 2:13; Hebrews 9:28). Scripture urges us to be watching, waiting, and ready for our Lord to return. Every day that passes brings us one day closer. Whether He returns next week or 100 years from now, we are to be living as though He were coming today.

Anticipation Is Key

Anticipation is the key to preparation. If you were expecting an important visitor, you would probably make proper preparation for his visit and keep looking for him to arrive. Your anticipation of the visitor's arrival would influence your preparation for his visit. The same is true of our anticipation of the coming of Christ. If we really believe He is coming, we will want to be prepared for Him when He comes.

Jesus illustrated this in His own prophetic teaching with the story of the ten virgins (Matthew 25:1-13). Only those who were prepared for the wedding were invited into the wedding banquet.

The others were left out. Jesus used this illustration to remind us to "keep watching" because we don't know the time of His coming. Dr. John Walvoord makes this comment: "The important point here… is that preparation should precede the second coming of Christ and that it will be too late when He comes."[8]

If we can take seriously the biblical predictions about the end time, then we must make preparation now for what is coming in the future. We cannot wait until all other options have been exhausted. The time for action is now. If you are not sure about your own relationship with Christ, make sure before it is too late.

Many things demand our attention in life. Many voices are calling to us, and many images flash across our minds. But regardless of our focus in life, one thing is certain: All of us will face death at some point. We cannot avoid it. All of us are vulnerable.

Death is the great equalizer. It makes no difference how rich or poor, famous or infamous, respected or rejected you may have been in this life. When you face death, you are facing an impartial judge. The Bible reminds us that "all have sinned" (Romans 3:23) and the "wages of sin is death" (Romans 6:23). When death comes knocking at your door, all that really matters is that you are ready to face it.

Jesus came the first time to pay the price for our sins so that we might be forgiven. He is called our Redeemer because He has redeemed us from God's judgment against our sin. "You were redeemed…with the precious blood of Christ…He was chosen before the creation of the world, but was revealed in these last times for your sake" (1 Peter 1:18-20 NIV).

In the meantime, we can live with our eyes looking to the skies, watching for Christ to come, and with our feet on the earth, working for Him until He comes. We are to balance expectation (the awareness that Jesus could come at any moment) with participation (serving Him faithfully until He comes). Living in the light of His coming keeps us focused on what is really important in life.

25 AMAZING PROPHECIES OF THE END TIMES

The prophecies in this appendix are listed in 25 categories and taken directly from the New International Version of the Bible. These are for personal study and easy cross-reference. The Bible is the only source of the "sure word of prophecy" (2 Peter 1:19 KJV). And God's Word is the only true prophecy of future events. More important than human opinion is what God says about the future. Search these scriptures for yourself and see what the Holy Spirit has revealed about the end times.

1. *Spread of the Gospel Message and Growth of the Church*

"I will build my church, and the gates of Hades will not overcome it" (Matthew 16:18).

"This gospel of the kingdom will be preached in the whole world as a testimony to all nations, and then the end will come" (Matthew 24:14).

"The kingdom of heaven is like a mustard seed, which a man

took and planted in his field. Though it is the smallest of all seeds, yet when it grows, it is the largest of garden plants and becomes a tree" (Matthew 13:31-32).

2. *Increase of Wickedness and the Spread of Evil*

"Because of the increase of wickedness, the love of most will grow cold" (Matthew 24:12).

"But mark this: There will be terrible times in the last days. People will be lovers of themselves, lovers of money, boastful, proud, abusive, disobedient to their parents, ungrateful, unholy, without love, unforgiving, slanderous, without self-control, brutal, not lovers of the good, treacherous, rash, conceited, lovers of pleasure rather than lovers of God—having a form of godliness but denying its power" (2 Timothy 3:1-5).

"You must understand that in the last days scoffers will come, scoffing and following their own evil desires. They will say, 'Where is this "coming" he promised?'" (2 Peter 3:3-4).

"Remember what the apostles of our Lord Jesus Christ foretold. They said to you, 'In the last times there will be scoffers who will follow their own ungodly desires'" (Jude 17-18).

3. *Rise of False Prophets and Apostate Religion*

"The Spirit clearly says that in later times some will abandon the faith and follow deceiving spirits and things taught by demons" (1 Timothy 4:1).

"Jesus answered: 'Watch out that no one deceives you. For many will come in my name, claiming, "I am the Messiah," and will deceive many...For false messiahs and false prophets will appear and perform great signs and wonders to deceive, if possible, even the elect'" (Matthew 24:4-5,24).

"There were also false prophets among the people, just as there will be false teachers among you. They will secretly introduce destructive heresies...In their greed these teachers will exploit you with fabricated stories" (2 Peter 2:1-3).

"For such people are false apostles, deceitful workers, masquerading as apostles of Christ. And no wonder, for Satan himself masquerades as an angel of light" (2 Corinthians 11:13-14).

4. *Continuation of "the Times of the Gentiles"*

"Jerusalem will be trampled on by the Gentiles until the times of the Gentiles are fulfilled" (Luke 21:24).

"I do not want you to be ignorant of this mystery, brothers... Israel has experienced a hardening in part until the full number of the Gentiles has come in" (Romans 11:25).

"I ask then: Did God reject his people? By no means!...at the present time there is a remnant chosen by grace" (Romans 11:1,5).

"How long will it be before these astonishing things are fulfilled?... 'It will be for a time, times and half a time. When the power of the holy people has been finally broken, all these things will be completed'" (Daniel 12:6-7).

5. *Return of Israel to the Land*

"I will bring you from the nations and gather you from the countries where you have been scattered" (Ezekiel 20:34).

"Therefore prophesy and say to them: 'This is what the Sovereign LORD says: O my people, I am going to open your graves and bring you up from them; I will bring you back to the land of Israel...and I will settle you in your own land'" (Ezekiel 37:12,14).

"This is what the Sovereign LORD says: 'I will take the Israelites out of the nations where they have gone. I will gather them from all around and bring them back into their own land'" (Ezekiel 37:21).

"I will bring your children from the east and gather you from the west. I will say to the north, 'Give them up!' and to the south, 'Do not hold them back.' Bring my sons from afar and my daughters from the ends of the earth" (Isaiah 43:5-6).

"I will bring back my exiled people Israel; they will rebuild the ruined cities and live in them" (Amos 9:14).

6. *Conflict in the Middle East*

"When you see Jerusalem being surrounded by armies, you will know that its desolation is near...For this is the time of punishment in fulfillment of all that has been written" (Luke 21:20,22).

"The word of the LORD came to me: 'Son of man, set your face against Gog, of the land of Magog, the chief prince of Meshek and Tubal...Persia, Cush and Put will be with them...also Gomer will all its troops, and Beth Togarmah from the far north with all its troops—the many nations with you'" (Ezekiel 38:1-2,5-6).

"I will gather all nations and bring them down to the Valley of Jehoshaphat...Proclaim this among the nations: Prepare for war!...Multitudes, multitudes in the valley of decision! For the day of the LORD is near in the valley of decision" (Joel 3:2,9,14).

"You will hear of wars and rumors of wars, but see to it that you are not alarmed. Such things must happen, but the end is still to come. Nation will rise against nation, and kingdom against kingdom" (Matthew 24:6-7).

7. *The Rapture of the Church*

"If I go and prepare a place for you, I will come back and take you to be with me that you also may be where I am" (John 14:3).

"I will also keep you from the hour of trial that is going to come on the whole world" (Revelation 3:10).

"Concerning the coming of our Lord Jesus Christ and our being gathered to him, we ask you, brothers and sisters, not to become easily unsettled or alarmed" (2 Thessalonians 2:1-2).

"The dead in Christ will rise first. After that, we who are still alive and are left will be caught up together with them in the clouds to meet the Lord in the air" (1 Thessalonians 4:16-17).

"Listen, I tell you a mystery: We will not all sleep, but we will all be changed—in a flash, in the twinkling of an eye, at the last trumpet. For the trumpet will sound, the dead will be raised imperishable, and we will be changed" (1 Corinthians 15:51-52).

"They came to life and reigned with Christ a thousand years... This is the first resurrection" (Revelation 20:4-5).

8. *Marriage of Christ and the Church in Heaven*

"Let us rejoice and be glad and give him glory! For the wedding of the Lamb has come, and his bride has made herself ready" (Revelation 19:7).

"I am jealous for you with a godly jealousy. I promised you to one husband, to Christ, so that I might present you as a pure virgin to him" (2 Corinthians 11:2).

"Husbands, love your wives, just as Christ loved the church and gave himself up for her to make her holy...and to present her to himself as a radiant church, without stain or wrinkle or any other blemish, but holy and blameless" (Ephesians 5:25-27).

"At midnight the cry rang out: 'Here's the bridegroom! Come out to meet him!' " (Matthew 25:6).

9. *Rise of the Antichrist and the False Prophet*

"Don't let anyone deceive you in any way, for that day will not come until the rebellion occurs and the man of lawlessness is revealed, the man doomed to destruction. He will oppose and will exalt himself over everything that is called God or is worshiped, so that he sets himself up in God's temple, proclaiming himself to be God…And then the lawless one will be revealed, whom the Lord Jesus will overthrow with the breath of his mouth and destroy by the splendor of his coming" (2 Thessalonians 2:3-4,8).

"Who is the liar? It is whoever denies that Jesus is the Christ. Such a person is the antichrist—denying the Father and the Son" (1 John 2:22).

"I saw a beast coming out of the sea. It had ten horns and seven heads…resembled a leopard…a bear…a lion. The dragon gave the beast his power and his throne and great authority…The whole world was filled with wonder and followed the beast… and they also worshiped the beast and asked, 'Who is like the beast? Who can make war against it?'" (Revelation 13:1-4).

"I saw a second beast, coming out of the earth. It had two horns like a lamb, but it spoke like a dragon. It…made the earth and its inhabitants worship the first beast…it deceived the inhabitants of the earth. It ordered them to set up an image in honor of the beast…It also forced all people, great and small, rich and poor, free and slave, to receive a mark on their right hands or on their foreheads, so that they could not buy or sell unless they had the mark, which is the name of the beast or the number of its name…666" (Revelation 13:11-12,14-18).

10. *Development of a Global Economy*

"It also forced all people, great and small, rich and poor, free and slave, to receive a mark on their right hands or on their foreheads so that they could not buy or sell unless they had the mark, which is the name of the beast or the number of its name" (Revelation 13:16-17).

"The merchants of the earth grew rich from [Babylon's] excessive luxuries…The merchants of the earth will weep and mourn over her because no one buys their cargoes anymore—cargoes of gold, silver, precious stones and pearls; fine linen, purple, silk and scarlet cloth; every sort of citron wood, and articles of every kind made of ivory, costly wood, bronze, iron and marble…Your merchants were the world's important people. By your magic spell all the nations were led astray" (Revelation 18:3,11-12,23).

11. *Formation of a World Government*

"It will be different from all the other kingdoms and will devour the whole earth, trampling it down and crushing it" (Daniel 7:23).

"All inhabitants of the earth will worship the beast—all whose names have not been written in the Lamb's book of life, the Lamb who was slain from the creation of the world" (Revelation 13:8).

"It exercised all the authority of the first beast on its behalf, and made the earth and its inhabitants worship the first beast, whose fatal wound had been healed" (Revelation 13:12).

"Come, I will show you…the great prostitute, who sits by many waters…The waters you saw, where the prostitute sits, are peoples, multitudes, nations and languages…the woman you saw is the great city that rules over the kings of the earth" (Revelation 17:1,15,18).

12. *Sense of False Peace and Security*

"'Peace, peace,' they say, when there is no peace" (Jeremiah 6:14).

"You know very well that the day of the Lord will come like a thief in the night. While people are saying, 'Peace and safety,' destruction will come on them suddenly, as labor pains on a pregnant woman, and they will not escape" (1 Thessalonians 5:2-3).

13. *Development of Weapons of Mass Destruction*

"Another horse came out, a fiery red one. Its rider was given power to take peace from the earth and to make people kill each other. To him was given a large sword" (Revelation 6:4).

"The sun turned black like sackcloth made of goat hair, the whole moon turned blood red, and the stars in the sky fell to earth…The heavens receded like a scroll being rolled up, and every mountain and island was removed from its place" (Revelation 6:12-14).

"The day of the Lord will come like a thief. The heavens will disappear with a roar; the elements will be destroyed by fire, and the earth and everything in it will be laid bare" (2 Peter 3:10).

"The first angel sounded his trumpet, and there came hail and fire mixed with blood, and it was hurled down on the earth. A third of the earth was burned up, a third of the trees were burned up, and all the green grass was burned up" (Revelation 8:7).

"The number of the mounted troops was twice ten thousand times ten thousand…out of their mouths came fire, smoke and sulfur. A third of mankind was killed by the three plagues of fire, smoke and sulfur that came out of their mouths" (Revelation 9:16-18).

14. *Environmental Disasters*

"Something like a huge mountain, all ablaze, was thrown into the sea…a third of the living creatures in the sea died…a great star, blazing like a torch, fell from the sky…A third of the waters turned bitter, and many people died…the sun was struck…the moon…the stars…A third of the day was without light, and also a third of the night" (Revelation 8:8-12).

"Ugly, festering sores broke out on the people…the sea… turned into blood…and every living thing in the sea died… the rivers and springs of water…became blood…the sun was allowed to scorch people with fire…and they cursed the name of God" (Revelation 16:2-4,8-9).

15. *Judgments of the Tribulation Period*

"There will be a time of distress such as has not happened from the beginning of nations until then" (Daniel 12:1).

"The great day of the LORD is near—near and coming quickly… That day will be a day of wrath—a day of distress and anguish, a day of trouble and ruin, a day of darkness and gloom, a day of clouds and blackness…In the fire of his jealousy the whole world will be consumed, for he will make a sudden end of all who live on the earth" (Zephaniah 1:14-15,18).

"There will be great distress, unequaled from the beginning of the world until now—and never to be equaled again. If those days had not been cut short, no one would survive, but for the sake of the elect those days will be shortened" (Matthew 24:21-22).

"How awful that day will be! No other will be like it. It will be a time of trouble for Jacob, but he will be saved out of it" (Jeremiah 30:7).

"See, the LORD is going to lay waste the earth and devastate it; he will ruin its face and scatter its inhabitants…The earth is broken up, the earth is split asunder, the earth is violently shaken. The earth reels like a drunkard, it sways like a hut in the wind" (Isaiah 24:1,19-20).

"You know very well that the day of the Lord will come like a thief in the night. While people are saying, 'Peace and safety,' destruction will come on them suddenly, as labor pains on a pregnant woman, and they will not escape" (1 Thessalonians 5:1-3).

"They called to the mountains and the rocks, 'Fall on us and hide us from the face of him who sits on the throne and from the wrath of the Lamb! For the great day of their wrath has come and who can withstand it?'" (Revelation 6:16-17).

16. *Conversion of Israel*

"I will make known my holy name among my people Israel...It is coming! It will surely take place, declares the Sovereign LORD. This is the day I have spoken of" (Ezekiel 39:7-8).

"I will pour out on the house of David and the inhabitants of Jerusalem a spirit of grace and supplication. They will look on me, the one they have pierced, and they will mourn for him as one mourns for an only child, and grieve bitterly for him as one grieves for a firstborn son" (Zechariah 12:10).

"On that day a fountain will be opened to the house of David and the inhabitants of Jerusalem, to cleanse them from sin and impurity...If someone asks, 'What are these wounds on your body?' they will answer, 'The wounds I was given at the house of my friends'" (Zechariah 13:1,6).

"Israel has experienced a hardening in part until the full number of Gentiles has come in, and in this way all Israel will be saved. As it is written: 'The deliverer will come from Zion; he will turn godlessness away from Jacob. And this is my covenant with them when I take away their sins'" (Romans 11:25-27).

"I heard the number of those who were sealed: 144,000 from all the tribes of Israel" (Revelation 7:4).

17. *Battle of Armageddon*

"They gathered the kings together to the place that in Hebrew is called Armageddon" (Revelation 16:16).

"See, the LORD is going to lay waste the earth and devastate it... Therefore earth's inhabitants are burned up, and very few are left" (Isaiah 24:1,6).

"The LORD is angry with all nations; his wrath is on all their armies. He will totally destroy them...the mountains will be soaked with their blood" (Isaiah 34:2-3).

"The LORD will strike all the nations that fought against Jerusalem: Their flesh will rot while they are still standing on their feet, their eyes will rot in their sockets, and their tongues will rot in their mouths. On that day people will be stricken by the LORD with great panic" (Zechariah 14:12-13).

"The beast was captured, and with it the false prophet...The two of them were thrown alive into the fiery lake of burning sulfur" (Revelation 19:20).

18. *Fall of Babylon*

"Fallen! Fallen is Babylon the Great! She has become a dwelling for demons and a haunt for every impure spirit...Give her as much torment and grief as the glory and luxury she gave herself...Therefore in one day her plagues will overtake her: death, mourning and famine. She will be consumed by fire, for mighty is the LORD God who judges her. When the kings of the earth... see the smoke of her burning, they will weep and mourn over her...Woe! Woe to you, great city, you mighty city of Babylon! In one hour your doom has come!" (Revelation 18:2,7-10).

"With such violence the great city of Babylon will be thrown down, never to be found again" (Revelation 18:21).

19. *Judgment Seat of Christ*

"We will all stand before God's judgment seat...So then, each of us will give an account of ourselves to God" (Romans 14:10,12).

"We must all appear before the judgment seat of Christ, so that each of us may receive what is due us for the things done while in the body, whether good or bad" (2 Corinthians 5:10).

"Their work will be shown for what it is...It will be revealed with fire, and the fire will test the quality of each person's work...If it is burned up, the builder will suffer loss but yet will be saved—even though only as one escaping through the flames" (1 Corinthians 3:13-15).

"I have fought the good fight, I have finished the race, I have kept the faith. Now there is in store for me the crown of righteousness, which the Lord, the righteous Judge, will award to me on that day—and not only to me, but also to all who have longed for his appearing" (2 Timothy 4:7-8).

20. *Triumphal Return of Christ and His Church*

"There will be signs in the sun, moon and stars...heavenly bodies will be shaken. At that time they will see the Son of Man coming in a cloud with power and great glory. When these things begin to take place, stand up and lift up your heads, because your redemption is drawing near" (Luke 21:25-28).

"Then will appear the sign of the Son of Man in heaven. And then all the peoples of the earth will mourn when they see the Son of Man coming on the clouds of heaven, with power and great glory" (Matthew 24:30).

"The Lord will go out and fight against those nations...On that day his feet will stand on the Mount of Olives, east of Jerusalem, and the Mount of Olives will be split in two from east to west" (Zechariah 14:3-4).

"Who is this coming from Edom, from Bozrah, with his garments stained crimson? Who is this, robed in splendor, striding forward in the greatness of his strength?...I trampled them in my anger and trod them down in my wrath; their blood spattered my garments, and I stained all my clothing. It was for me the day of vengeance; the year for me to redeem had come" (Isaiah 63:1,3-4).

"Multitudes, multitudes in the valley of decision! For the day of the Lord is near in the valley of decision. The sun and moon will be darkened, and the stars no longer shine. The Lord will roar from Zion and thunder from Jerusalem; the earth and the heavens will tremble. But the LORD will be a refuge for his people, a stronghold for the people of Israel" (Joel 3:14-16).

"I saw heaven standing open and there before me was a white horse, whose rider is called Faithful and True. With justice he judges and wages war. His eyes are like blazing fire, and on his head are many crowns. He has a name written on him that no one knows but he himself. He is dressed in a robe dipped in blood, and his name is the Word of God. The armies of heaven were following him, riding on white horses and dressed in fine linen, white and clean. Coming out of his mouth is a sharp sword with which to strike down the nations. He will rule them with an iron scepter. He treads the winepress of the fury of the wrath of God Almighty. On his robe and on his thigh he has this name written: King of kings and Lord of lords" (Revelation 19:11-16).

21. *Judgment of the Nations*

"In those days and at that time, when I restore the fortunes of Judah and Jerusalem, I will gather all nations and bring them down to the Valley of Jehoshaphat. There I will put them on trial for what they did to my inheritance, my people Israel" (Joel 3:1-2).

"When the Son of Man comes in his glory, and all the angels with him, he will sit on his glorious throne. All the nations will be gathered before him, and he will separate the people one from another as a shepherd separates the sheep from the goats. He will put the sheep on his right and the goats on his left. Then the King will say to those on his right, 'Come, you who are blessed by my Father; take your inheritance, the kingdom prepared for you since the creation of the world'... Then he will say to those on his left, 'Depart from me, you who are cursed, into the eternal fire prepared for the devil and his angels' " (Matthew 25:31-34,41).

22. *Millennial Kingdom*

"The beast was captured, and with him the false prophet...The two of them were thrown alive into the fiery lake of burning sulfur...And I saw an angel coming down out of heaven, having the key to the Abyss and holding in his hand a great chain. He seized the dragon, that ancient serpent, who is the devil, or Satan, and bound him for a thousand years...into the Abyss" (Revelation 19:20; 20:1-3).

"You have made them to be a kingdom and priests to serve our God, and they will reign on the earth" (Revelation 5:10).

"They came to life and reigned with Christ a thousand years... This is the first resurrection...The second death has no power over them, but they will be priests of God and of Christ and will reign with him for a thousand years" (Revelation 20:4-6).

"In the last days the mountain of the LORD's temple will be established as the highest of the mountains; it will be exalted above the hills, and all nations will stream to it. Many peoples will come and say, 'Come, let us go up to the mountain of the LORD, to the house of the God of Jacob'...The law will go out from Zion, the word of the LORD from Jerusalem...They will beat their swords into plowshares and their spears into pruning hooks. Nation will not take up sword against nation, nor will they train for war anymore" (Isaiah 2:2-4).

"For to us a child is born, to us a son is given, and the government will be on his shoulders. And he will be called Wonderful Counselor, Mighty God, Everlasting Father, Prince of Peace. Of the greatness of his government and peace there will be no end. He will reign on David's throne and over his kingdom, establishing and upholding it with justice and righteousness from that time on and forever" (Isaiah 9:6-7).

23. *Great White Throne Judgment*

"When the thousand years are over, Satan will be released from his prison and will go out to deceive the nations...to gather them for battle...But fire came down from heaven and devoured them. And the devil, who deceived them, was thrown into the lake of burning sulfur, where the beast and the false prophet had been thrown. They will be tormented day and night for ever and ever.

Then I saw a great white throne and him who was seated on it. The earth and the heavens fled from his presence, and there was no place for them. And I saw the dead, great and small, standing before the throne, and books were opened. Another book was opened, which is the book of life...death and Hades gave up the dead that were in them, and each person was judged according to what they had done. Then death and Hades were thrown into the lake of fire. The lake of fire is the second death. Anyone whose name was not found written in the book of life was thrown into the lake of fire" (Revelation 20:7-15).

24. *New Heavens and New Earth*

"See, I will create new heavens and a new earth. The former things will not be remembered, nor will they come to mind...I will rejoice over Jerusalem and take delight in my people; the sound of weeping and of crying will be heard in it no more...This is what the LORD says: 'Heaven is my throne, and the earth is my footstool. Where is the house you will build for me? Where will my resting place be? Has not my hand made all these things, and so they came into being?'" (Isaiah 65:17,19; 66:1-2).

"I saw a new heaven and a new earth, for the first heaven and the first earth had passed away, and there was no longer any sea. I saw the Holy City, the new Jerusalem, coming down out of heaven from God, prepared as a bride...One of the seven angels...said to me, 'Come, I will show you the bride, the wife of the Lamb.' And he...showed me the Holy City, Jerusalem, coming down out of heaven from God. It shone with the glory of God'…I did not see a temple in the city, because the Lord God Almighty and the Lamb are its temple. The city does not need the sun or the moon to shine on it, for the glory of God gives it light, and the Lamb is its lamp" (Revelation 21:1-2,9-11,22-23).

25. *Eternal State*

"Multitudes who sleep in the dust of the earth will awake: some to everlasting life, others to shame and everlasting contempt. Those who are wise will shine like the brightness of the heavens, and those who lead many to righteousness, like the stars for ever and ever" (Daniel 12:2-3).

"Your dead will live, LORD; their bodies will rise—let those who dwell in the dust, wake up and shout for joy" (Isaiah 26:19).

"Jesus said to her, 'I am the resurrection and the life. The one who believes in me will live, even though they die; and whoever lives and believes in me will never die'" (John 11:25-26).

"Then the end will come, when he hands over the kingdom to God the Father after he has destroyed all dominion, authority, and power. For he must reign until he has put all his enemies under his feet. The last enemy to be destroyed is death… When the perishable has been clothed with the imperishable, and the mortal with immortality, then the saying that is written will come true: 'Death has been swallowed up in victory'" (1 Corinthians 15:24-26,54).

"I heard a loud voice from the throne saying, 'Look! God's dwelling place is now among the people, and he will dwell with them. They will be his people, and God himself will be with them and be their God. He will wipe every tear from their eyes. There will be no more death or mourning or crying or pain, for the old order of things has passed away'" (Revelation 21:3-4).

"The angel showed me the river of the water of life, as clear as crystal, flowing from the throne of God and of the Lamb…On each side of the river stood the tree of life…The throne of God and of the Lamb will be in the city, and his servants will serve him. They will see his face, and his name will be on their foreheads…And they will reign for ever and ever" (Revelation 22:1-5).

"Whoever believes in the Son has eternal life, but whoever rejects the Son will not see life, for God's wrath remains on them" (John 3:36).

"Everyone who calls on the name of the Lord will be saved" (Romans 10:13).

Notes

Chapter 2: Understanding Bible Prophecy

1. Paul N. Benware, *Understanding End Times Prophecy* (Chicago: Moody Press, 2006), pp. 19-29.

Chapter 3: Are We Living in the Last Days?

1. Charles Colson, *Against the Night* (Ann Arbor: Servant, 1989), p. 55.

2. *The European*, October 11, 1991, p. 1.

Chapter 7: Beware of False Prophets

1. J. Hampton Keathley, III, "The Beast and the False Prophet," Bible.org. Accessed at http://bible.org/seriespage/beast-and-false-prophet-rev-131-18.

2. John Walvoord, "The Beasts and the False Prophet," Bible.org. Accessed at http://bible.org/seriespage/13-beasts-and-false-prophet.

Chapter 10: The Battle of Armageddon

1. Arnold Fruchtenbaum, *Footsteps of the Messiah: A Study of the Sequence of Prophetic Events* (Tustin: Ariel Press, 2003).

2. Ibid, p. 314.

3. Ibid, p. 337.

A Final Word: Until He Comes

1. Erwin Lutzer, *Where Do We Go from Here?* (Chicago: Moody Press, 1993), pp. 25-48.

2. Bill Hybels, *Becoming a Contagious Christian* (Grand Rapids: Zondervan, 1994), pp. 43,59.

3. Dave Hunt, *Whatever Happened to Heaven?* (Eugene: Harvest House, 1988), p. 7.

4. Joseph Stowell, "Set Your Mind on Heaven," in *10 Reasons Why Jesus Is Coming Soon* (Sisters: Multnomah Books, 1998), p. 235.

5. C.S. Lewis, *Mere Christianity* (New York: Macmillan, 1943), p. 118.

6. Quoted by Lutzer, p. 46.

7. Quoted by Lutzer, p. 47.

8. John Walvoord, *Matthew: Thy Kingdom Come* (Chicago: Moody Press, 1974), p. 197.

The Pre-Trib Research Center

In 1993, Dr. Tim LaHaye and Dr. Thomas Ice founded the Pre-Trib Research Center (PTRC) for the purpose of encouraging the research, teaching, propagation, and defense of the pretribulational rapture view, the literal interpretation of the Bible, and related Bible prophecy doctrines. The PTRC sponsors annual study-group meetings and has produced an impressive array of literature. Its members include top prophecy scholars, authors, Bible teachers, and prophecy students.

Pre-Trib Research Center
PO Box 21796
El Cajon, CA 92021
www.pre-trib.org
